50% Off CAST Test Prep Course!

By Mometrix

Dear Customer,

We consider it an honor and a privilege that you chose our CAST Study Guide. As a way of showing our appreciation and to help us better serve you, we are offering **50% off our online CAST Prep Course.** Many CAST courses are needlessly expensive and don't deliver enough value. With our course, you get access to the best CAST prep material, and **you only pay half price**.

We have structured our online course to perfectly complement your printed study guide. The CAST Test Prep Course contains **in-depth lessons** that cover all the most important topics, **20+ video reviews** that explain difficult concepts, over **350 practice questions** to ensure you feel prepared, and more than **50 flashcards** for studying on the go.

Online CAST Prep Course

Topics Include:

- Mechanical Concepts
  - Kinematics
  - Kinetics
  - Machines
- Reading Comprehension
  - Inference
  - Author's Attitude
  - Main Idea
- Mathematical Usage
  - Long Division
  - Multiplication
  - Decimals
  - Unit Conversions
- Graphic Arithmetic
  - Ratios
  - Distance

Course Features:

- CAST Study Guide
  - Get content that complements our best-selling study guide.
- Full-Length Practice Tests
  - With over 350 practice questions, you can test yourself again and again.
- Mobile Friendly
  - If you need to study on the go, the course is easily accessible from your mobile device.
- CAST Flashcards
  - Our course includes a flashcard mode consisting of over 50 content cards to help you study.

To receive this discount, visit our website at mometrix.com/university/cast or simply scan this QR code with your smartphone. At the checkout page, enter the discount code: **cast50off**

If you have any questions or concerns, please contact us at support@mometrix.com.

SCAN HERE

CAST

Exam Secrets
Study Guide

Written and edited by Mometrix Test Prep

Printed in the United States of America

This paper meets the requirements of ANSI/NISO Z39.48-1992 (Permanence of Paper).

Mometrix offers volume discount pricing to institutions. For more information or a price quote, please contact our sales department at sales@mometrix.com or 888-248-1219.

Paperback
ISBN 13: 978-1-5167-1608-1
ISBN 10: 1-5167-1608-6

DEAR FUTURE EXAM SUCCESS STORY

First of all, **THANK YOU** for purchasing Mometrix study materials!

Second, congratulations! You are one of the few determined test-takers who are committed to doing whatever it takes to excel on your exam. **You have come to the right place.** We developed these study materials with one goal in mind: to deliver you the information you need in a format that's concise and easy to use.

In addition to optimizing your guide for the content of the test, we've outlined our recommended steps for breaking down the preparation process into small, attainable goals so you can make sure you stay on track.

We've also analyzed the entire test-taking process, identifying the most common pitfalls and showing how you can overcome them and be ready for any curveball the test throws you.

Standardized testing is one of the biggest obstacles on your road to success, which only increases the importance of doing well in the high-pressure, high-stakes environment of test day. Your results on this test could have a significant impact on your future, and this guide provides the information and practical advice to help you achieve your full potential on test day.

Your success is our success

We would love to hear from you! If you would like to share the story of your exam success or if you have any questions or comments in regard to our products, please contact us at **800-673-8175** or **support@mometrix.com**.

Thanks again for your business and we wish you continued success!

Sincerely,
The Mometrix Test Preparation Team

> **Need more help? Check out our flashcards at:**
> **http://MometrixFlashcards.com/CAST**

TABLE OF CONTENTS

Introduction

Thank you for purchasing this resource! You have made the choice to prepare yourself for a test that could have a huge impact on your future, and this guide is designed to help you be fully ready for test day. Obviously, it's important to have a solid understanding of the test material, but you also need to be prepared for the unique environment and stressors of the test, so that you can perform to the best of your abilities.

For this purpose, the first section that appears in this guide is the **Secret Keys**. We've devoted countless hours to meticulously researching what works and what doesn't, and we've boiled down our findings to the five most impactful steps you can take to improve your performance on the test. We start at the beginning with study planning and move through the preparation process, all the way to the testing strategies that will help you get the most out of what you know when you're finally sitting in front of the test.

We recommend that you start preparing for your test as far in advance as possible. However, if you've bought this guide as a last-minute study resource and only have a few days before your test, we recommend that you skip over the first two Secret Keys since they address a long-term study plan.

If you struggle with **test anxiety**, we strongly encourage you to check out our recommendations for how you can overcome it. Test anxiety is a formidable foe, but it can be beaten, and we want to make sure you have the tools you need to defeat it.

1

Secret Key #1 – Plan Big, Study Small

There's a lot riding on your performance. If you want to ace this test, you're going to need to keep your skills sharp and the material fresh in your mind. You need a plan that lets you review everything you need to know while still fitting in your schedule. We'll break this strategy down into three categories.

Information Organization

Start with the information you already have: the official test outline. From this, you can make a complete list of all the concepts you need to cover before the test. Organize these concepts into groups that can be studied together, and create a list of any related vocabulary you need to learn so you can brush up on any difficult terms. You'll want to keep this vocabulary list handy once you actually start studying since you may need to add to it along the way.

Time Management

Once you have your set of study concepts, decide how to spread them out over the time you have left before the test. Break your study plan into small, clear goals so you have a manageable task for each day and know exactly what you're doing. Then just focus on one small step at a time. When you manage your time this way, you don't need to spend hours at a time studying. Studying a small block of content for a short period each day helps you retain information better and avoid stressing over how much you have left to do. You can relax knowing that you have a plan to cover everything in time. In order for this strategy to be effective though, you have to start studying early and stick to your schedule. Avoid the exhaustion and futility that comes from last-minute cramming!

Study Environment

The environment you study in has a big impact on your learning. Studying in a coffee shop, while probably more enjoyable, is not likely to be as fruitful as studying in a quiet room. It's important to keep distractions to a minimum. You're only planning to study for a short block of time, so make the most of it. Don't pause to check your phone or get up to find a snack. It's also important to **avoid multitasking**. Research has consistently shown that multitasking will make your studying dramatically less effective. Your study area should also be comfortable and well-lit so you don't have the distraction of straining your eyes or sitting on an uncomfortable chair.

 The time of day you study is also important. You want to be rested and alert. Don't wait until just before bedtime. Study when you'll be most likely to comprehend and remember. Even better, if you know what time of day your test will be, set that time aside for study. That way your brain will be used to working on that subject at that specific time and you'll have a better chance of recalling information.

Finally, it can be helpful to team up with others who are studying for the same test. Your actual studying should be done in as isolated an environment as possible, but the work of organizing the information and setting up the study plan can be divided up. In between study sessions, you can discuss with your teammates the concepts that you're all studying and quiz each other on the details. Just be sure that your teammates are as serious about the test as you are. If you find that your study time is being replaced with social time, you might need to find a new team.

Secret Key #2 – Make Your Studying Count

You're devoting a lot of time and effort to preparing for this test, so you want to be absolutely certain it will pay off. This means doing more than just reading the content and hoping you can remember it on test day. It's important to make every minute of study count. There are two main areas you can focus on to make your studying count.

Retention

It doesn't matter how much time you study if you can't remember the material. You need to make sure you are retaining the concepts. To check your retention of the information you're learning, try recalling it at later times with minimal prompting. Try carrying around flashcards and glance at one or two from time to time or ask a friend who's also studying for the test to quiz you.

To enhance your retention, look for ways to put the information into practice so that you can apply it rather than simply recalling it. If you're using the information in practical ways, it will be much easier to remember. Similarly, it helps to solidify a concept in your mind if you're not only reading it to yourself but also explaining it to someone else. Ask a friend to let you teach them about a concept you're a little shaky on (or speak aloud to an imaginary audience if necessary). As you try to summarize, define, give examples, and answer your friend's questions, you'll understand the concepts better and they will stay with you longer. Finally, step back for a big picture view and ask yourself how each piece of information fits with the whole subject. When you link the different concepts together and see them working together as a whole, it's easier to remember the individual components.

Finally, practice showing your work on any multi-step problems, even if you're just studying. Writing out each step you take to solve a problem will help solidify the process in your mind, and you'll be more likely to remember it during the test.

Modality

Modality simply refers to the means or method by which you study. Choosing a study modality that fits your own individual learning style is crucial. No two people learn best in exactly the same way, so it's important to know your strengths and use them to your advantage.

For example, if you learn best by visualization, focus on visualizing a concept in your mind and draw an image or a diagram. Try color-coding your notes, illustrating them, or creating symbols that will trigger your mind to recall a learned concept. If you learn best by hearing or discussing information, find a study partner who learns the same way or read aloud to yourself. Think about how to put the information in your own words. Imagine that you are giving a lecture on the topic and record yourself so you can listen to it later.

For any learning style, flashcards can be helpful. Organize the information so you can take advantage of spare moments to review. Underline key words or phrases. Use different colors for different categories. Mnemonic devices (such as creating a short list in which every item starts with the same letter) can also help with retention. Find what works best for you and use it to store the information in your mind most effectively and easily.

3

Secret Key #3 – Practice the Right Way

Your success on test day depends not only on how many hours you put into preparing, but also on whether you prepared the right way. It's good to check along the way to see if your studying is paying off. One of the most effective ways to do this is by taking practice tests to evaluate your progress. Practice tests are useful because they show exactly where you need to improve. Every time you take a practice test, pay special attention to these three groups of questions:

- The questions you got wrong
- The questions you had to guess on, even if you guessed right
- The questions you found difficult or slow to work through

This will show you exactly what your weak areas are, and where you need to devote more study time. Ask yourself why each of these questions gave you trouble. Was it because you didn't understand the material? Was it because you didn't remember the vocabulary? Do you need more repetitions on this type of question to build speed and confidence? Dig into those questions and figure out how you can strengthen your weak areas as you go back to review the material.

 Additionally, many practice tests have a section explaining the answer choices. It can be tempting to read the explanation and think that you now have a good understanding of the concept. However, an explanation likely only covers part of the question's broader context. Even if the explanation makes perfect sense, **go back and investigate** every concept related to the question until you're positive you have a thorough understanding.

As you go along, keep in mind that the practice test is just that: practice. Memorizing these questions and answers will not be very helpful on the actual test because it is unlikely to have any of the same exact questions. If you only know the right answers to the sample questions, you won't be prepared for the real thing. **Study the concepts** until you understand them fully, and then you'll be able to answer any question that shows up on the test.

It's important to wait on the practice tests until you're ready. If you take a test on your first day of study, you may be overwhelmed by the amount of material covered and how much you need to learn. Work up to it gradually.

On test day, you'll need to be prepared for answering questions, managing your time, and using the test-taking strategies you've learned. It's a lot to balance, like a mental marathon that will have a big impact on your future. Like training for a marathon, you'll need to start slowly and work your way up. When test day arrives, you'll be ready.

Start with the strategies you've read in the first two Secret Keys—plan your course and study in the way that works best for you. If you have time, consider using multiple study resources to get different approaches to the same concepts. It can be helpful to see difficult concepts from more than one angle. Then find a good source for practice tests. Many times, the test website will suggest potential study resources or provide sample tests.

Practice Test Strategy

If you're able to find at least three practice tests, we recommend this strategy:

UNTIMED AND OPEN-BOOK PRACTICE

Take the first test with no time constraints and with your notes and study guide handy. Take your time and focus on applying the strategies you've learned.

TIMED AND OPEN-BOOK PRACTICE

Take the second practice test open-book as well, but set a timer and practice pacing yourself to finish in time.

TIMED AND CLOSED-BOOK PRACTICE

Take any other practice tests as if it were test day. Set a timer and put away your study materials. Sit at a table or desk in a quiet room, imagine yourself at the testing center, and answer questions as quickly and accurately as possible.

Keep repeating timed and closed-book tests on a regular basis until you run out of practice tests or it's time for the actual test. Your mind will be ready for the schedule and stress of test day, and you'll be able to focus on recalling the material you've learned.

Secret Key #4 – Pace Yourself

Once you're fully prepared for the material on the test, your biggest challenge on test day will be managing your time. Just knowing that the clock is ticking can make you panic even if you have plenty of time left. Work on pacing yourself so you can build confidence against the time constraints of the exam. Pacing is a difficult skill to master, especially in a high-pressure environment, so **practice is vital**.

Set time expectations for your pace based on how much time is available. For example, if a section has 60 questions and the time limit is 30 minutes, you know you have to average 30 seconds or less per question in order to answer them all. Although 30 seconds is the hard limit, set 25 seconds per question as your goal, so you reserve extra time to spend on harder questions. When you budget extra time for the harder questions, you no longer have any reason to stress when those questions take longer to answer.

Don't let this time expectation distract you from working through the test at a calm, steady pace, but keep it in mind so you don't spend too much time on any one question. Recognize that taking extra time on one question you don't understand may keep you from answering two that you do understand later in the test. If your time limit for a question is up and you're still not sure of the answer, mark it and move on, and come back to it later if the time and the test format allow. If the testing format doesn't allow you to return to earlier questions, just make an educated guess; then put it out of your mind and move on.

On the easier questions, be careful not to rush. It may seem wise to hurry through them so you have more time for the challenging ones, but it's not worth missing one if you know the concept and just didn't take the time to read the question fully. Work efficiently but make sure you understand the question and have looked at all of the answer choices, since more than one may seem right at first.

Even if you're paying attention to the time, you may find yourself a little behind at some point. You should speed up to get back on track, but do so wisely. Don't panic; just take a few seconds less on each question until you're caught up. Don't guess without thinking, but do look through the answer choices and eliminate any you know are wrong. If you can get down to two choices, it is often worthwhile to guess from those. Once you've chosen an answer, move on and don't dwell on any that you skipped or had to hurry through. If a question was taking too long, chances are it was one of the harder ones, so you weren't as likely to get it right anyway.

On the other hand, if you find yourself getting ahead of schedule, it may be beneficial to slow down a little. The more quickly you work, the more likely you are to make a careless mistake that will affect your score. You've budgeted time for each question, so don't be afraid to spend that time. Practice an efficient but careful pace to get the most out of the time you have.

Secret Key #5 – Have a Plan for Guessing

When you're taking the test, you may find yourself stuck on a question. Some of the answer choices seem better than others, but you don't see the one answer choice that is obviously correct. What do you do?

The scenario described above is very common, yet most test takers have not effectively prepared for it. Developing and practicing a plan for guessing may be one of the single most effective uses of your time as you get ready for the exam.

In developing your plan for guessing, there are three questions to address:

- When should you start the guessing process?
- How should you narrow down the choices?
- Which answer should you choose?

When to Start the Guessing Process

Unless your plan for guessing is to select C every time (which, despite its merits, is not what we recommend), you need to leave yourself enough time to apply your answer elimination strategies. Since you have a limited amount of time for each question, that means that if you're going to give yourself the best shot at guessing correctly, you have to decide quickly whether or not you will guess.

Of course, the best-case scenario is that you don't have to guess at all, so first, see if you can answer the question based on your knowledge of the subject and basic reasoning skills. Focus on the key words in the question and try to jog your memory of related topics. Give yourself a chance to bring the knowledge to mind, but once you realize that you don't have (or you can't access) the knowledge you need to answer the question, it's time to start the guessing process.

It's almost always better to start the guessing process too early than too late. It only takes a few seconds to remember something and answer the question from knowledge. Carefully eliminating wrong answer choices takes longer. Plus, going through the process of eliminating answer choices can actually help jog your memory.

Summary: Start the guessing process as soon as you decide that you can't answer the question based on your knowledge.

How to Narrow Down the Choices

The next chapter in this book (**Test-Taking Strategies**) includes a wide range of strategies for how to approach questions and how to look for answer choices to eliminate. You will definitely want to read those carefully, practice them, and figure out which ones work best for you. Here though, we're going to address a mindset rather than a particular strategy.

Your odds of guessing an answer correctly depend on how many options you are choosing from.

Number of options left	5	4	3	2	1
Odds of guessing correctly	20%	25%	33%	50%	100%

You can see from this chart just how valuable it is to be able to eliminate incorrect answers and make an educated guess, but there are two things that many test takers do that cause them to miss out on the benefits of guessing:

- Accidentally eliminating the correct answer
- Selecting an answer based on an impression

We'll look at the first one here, and the second one in the next section.

To avoid accidentally eliminating the correct answer, we recommend a thought exercise called **the $5 challenge**. In this challenge, you only eliminate an answer choice from contention if you are willing to bet $5 on it being wrong. Why $5? Five dollars is a small but not insignificant amount of money. It's an amount you could afford to lose but wouldn't want to throw away. And while losing

$5 once might not hurt too much, doing it twenty times will set you back $100. In the same way, each small decision you make—eliminating a choice here, guessing on a question there—won't by itself impact your score very much, but when you put them all together, they can make a big difference. By holding each answer choice elimination decision to a higher standard, you can reduce the risk of accidentally eliminating the correct answer.

The $5 challenge can also be applied in a positive sense: If you are willing to bet $5 that an answer choice *is* correct, go ahead and mark it as correct.

Summary: Only eliminate an answer choice if you are willing to bet $5 that it is wrong.

Which Answer to Choose

You're taking the test. You've run into a hard question and decided you'll have to guess. You've eliminated all the answer choices you're willing to bet $5 on. Now you have to pick an answer. Why do we even need to talk about this? Why can't you just pick whichever one you feel like when the time comes?

The answer to these questions is that if you don't come into the test with a plan, you'll rely on your impression to select an answer choice, and if you do that, you risk falling into a trap. The test writers know that everyone who takes their test will be guessing on some of the questions, so they intentionally write wrong answer choices to seem plausible. You still have to pick an answer though, and if the wrong answer choices are designed to look right, how can you ever be sure that you're not falling for their trap? The best solution we've found to this dilemma is to take the decision out of your hands entirely. Here is the process we recommend:

Once you've eliminated any choices that you are confident (willing to bet $5) are wrong, select the first remaining choice as your answer.

Whether you choose to select the first remaining choice, the second, or the last, the important thing is that you use some preselected standard. Using this approach guarantees that you will not be enticed into selecting an answer choice that looks right, because you are not basing your decision on how the answer choices look.

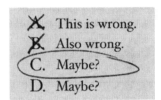

This is not meant to make you question your knowledge. Instead, it is to help you recognize the difference between your knowledge and your impressions. There's a huge difference between thinking an answer is right because of what you know, and thinking an answer is right because it looks or sounds like it should be right.

Summary: To ensure that your selection is appropriately random, make a predetermined selection from among all answer choices you have not eliminated.

Test-Taking Strategies

This section contains a list of test-taking strategies that you may find helpful as you work through the test. By taking what you know and applying logical thought, you can maximize your chances of answering any question correctly!

It is very important to realize that every question is different and every person is different: no single strategy will work on every question, and no single strategy will work for every person. That's why we've included all of them here, so you can try them out and determine which ones work best for different types of questions and which ones work best for you.

Question Strategies

⊘ READ CAREFULLY

Read the question and the answer choices carefully. Don't miss the question because you misread the terms. You have plenty of time to read each question thoroughly and make sure you understand what is being asked. Yet a happy medium must be attained, so don't waste too much time. You must read carefully and efficiently.

⊘ CONTEXTUAL CLUES

Look for contextual clues. If the question includes a word you are not familiar with, look at the immediate context for some indication of what the word might mean. Contextual clues can often give you all the information you need to decipher the meaning of an unfamiliar word. Even if you can't determine the meaning, you may be able to narrow down the possibilities enough to make a solid guess at the answer to the question.

⊘ PREFIXES

If you're having trouble with a word in the question or answer choices, try dissecting it. Take advantage of every clue that the word might include. Prefixes can be a huge help. Usually, they allow you to determine a basic meaning. *Pre-* means before, *post-* means after, *pro-* is positive, *de-* is negative. From prefixes, you can get an idea of the general meaning of the word and try to put it into context.

⊘ HEDGE WORDS

Watch out for critical hedge words, such as *likely, may, can, sometimes, often, almost, mostly, usually, generally, rarely,* and *sometimes.* Question writers insert these hedge phrases to cover every possibility. Often an answer choice will be wrong simply because it leaves no room for exception. Be on guard for answer choices that have definitive words such as *exactly* and *always.*

⊘ SWITCHBACK WORDS

Stay alert for *switchbacks.* These are the words and phrases frequently used to alert you to shifts in thought. The most common switchback words are *but, although,* and *however.* Others include *nevertheless, on the other hand, even though, while, in spite of, despite,* and *regardless of.* Switchback words are important to catch because they can change the direction of the question or an answer choice.

⊘ FACE VALUE

When in doubt, use common sense. Accept the situation in the problem at face value. Don't read too much into it. These problems will not require you to make wild assumptions. If you have to go beyond creativity and warp time or space in order to have an answer choice fit the question, then you should move on and consider the other answer choices. These are normal problems rooted in reality. The applicable relationship or explanation may not be readily apparent, but it is there for you to figure out. Use your common sense to interpret anything that isn't clear.

Answer Choice Strategies

⊘ ANSWER SELECTION

The most thorough way to pick an answer choice is to identify and eliminate wrong answers until only one is left, then confirm it is the correct answer. Sometimes an answer choice may immediately seem right, but be careful. The test writers will usually put more than one reasonable answer choice on each question, so take a second to read all of them and make sure that the other choices are not equally obvious. As long as you have time left, it is better to read every answer choice than to pick the first one that looks right without checking the others.

⊘ ANSWER CHOICE FAMILIES

An answer choice family consists of two (in rare cases, three) answer choices that are very similar in construction and cannot all be true at the same time. If you see two answer choices that are direct opposites or parallels, one of them is usually the correct answer. For instance, if one answer choice says that quantity x increases and another either says that quantity x decreases (opposite) or says that quantity y increases (parallel), then those answer choices would fall into the same family. An answer choice that doesn't match the construction of the answer choice family is more likely to be incorrect. Most questions will not have answer choice families, but when they do appear, you should be prepared to recognize them.

⊘ ELIMINATE ANSWERS

Eliminate answer choices as soon as you realize they are wrong, but make sure you consider all possibilities. If you are eliminating answer choices and realize that the last one you are left with is also wrong, don't panic. Start over and consider each choice again. There may be something you missed the first time that you will realize on the second pass.

⊘ AVOID FACT TRAPS

Don't be distracted by an answer choice that is factually true but doesn't answer the question. You are looking for the choice that answers the question. Stay focused on what the question is asking for so you don't accidentally pick an answer that is true but incorrect. Always go back to the question and make sure the answer choice you've selected actually answers the question and is not merely a true statement.

⊘ EXTREME STATEMENTS

In general, you should avoid answers that put forth extreme actions as standard practice or proclaim controversial ideas as established fact. An answer choice that states the "process should be used in certain situations, if…" is much more likely to be correct than one that states the "process should be discontinued completely." The first is a calm rational statement and doesn't even make a definitive, uncompromising stance, using a hedge word *if* to provide wiggle room, whereas the second choice is far more extreme.

11

⊘ Benchmark

As you read through the answer choices and you come across one that seems to answer the question well, mentally select that answer choice. This is not your final answer, but it's the one that will help you evaluate the other answer choices. The one that you selected is your benchmark or standard for judging each of the other answer choices. Every other answer choice must be compared to your benchmark. That choice is correct until proven otherwise by another answer choice beating it. If you find a better answer, then that one becomes your new benchmark. Once you've decided that no other choice answers the question as well as your benchmark, you have your final answer.

⊘ Predict the Answer

Before you even start looking at the answer choices, it is often best to try to predict the answer. When you come up with the answer on your own, it is easier to avoid distractions and traps because you will know exactly what to look for. The right answer choice is unlikely to be word-for-word what you came up with, but it should be a close match. Even if you are confident that you have the right answer, you should still take the time to read each option before moving on.

General Strategies

⊘ Tough Questions

If you are stumped on a problem or it appears too hard or too difficult, don't waste time. Move on! Remember though, if you can quickly check for obviously incorrect answer choices, your chances of guessing correctly are greatly improved. Before you completely give up, at least try to knock out a couple of possible answers. Eliminate what you can and then guess at the remaining answer choices before moving on.

⊘ Check Your Work

Since you will probably not know every term listed and the answer to every question, it is important that you get credit for the ones that you do know. Don't miss any questions through careless mistakes. If at all possible, try to take a second to look back over your answer selection and make sure you've selected the correct answer choice and haven't made a costly careless mistake (such as marking an answer choice that you didn't mean to mark). This quick double check should more than pay for itself in caught mistakes for the time it costs.

⊘ Pace Yourself

It's easy to be overwhelmed when you're looking at a page full of questions; your mind is confused and full of random thoughts, and the clock is ticking down faster than you would like. Calm down and maintain the pace that you have set for yourself. Especially as you get down to the last few minutes of the test, don't let the small numbers on the clock make you panic. As long as you are on track by monitoring your pace, you are guaranteed to have time for each question.

⊘ Don't Rush

It is very easy to make errors when you are in a hurry. Maintaining a fast pace in answering questions is pointless if it makes you miss questions that you would have gotten right otherwise. Test writers like to include distracting information and wrong answers that seem right. Taking a little extra time to avoid careless mistakes can make all the difference in your test score. Find a pace that allows you to be confident in the answers that you select.

⊘ Keep Moving

Panicking will not help you pass the test, so do your best to stay calm and keep moving. Taking deep breaths and going through the answer elimination steps you practiced can help to break through a stress barrier and keep your pace.

Final Notes

The combination of a solid foundation of content knowledge and the confidence that comes from practicing your plan for applying that knowledge is the key to maximizing your performance on test day. As your foundation of content knowledge is built up and strengthened, you'll find that the strategies included in this chapter become more and more effective in helping you quickly sift through the distractions and traps of the test to isolate the correct answer.

Now that you're preparing to move forward into the test content chapters of this book, be sure to keep your goal in mind. As you read, think about how you will be able to apply this information on the test. If you've already seen sample questions for the test and you have an idea of the question format and style, try to come up with questions of your own that you can answer based on what you're reading. This will give you valuable practice applying your knowledge in the same ways you can expect to on test day.

Good luck and good studying!

Introduction

Congratulations! You've decided to take the Construction and Skilled Trades (CAST) examination, which means you are pursuing employment as a construction worker or skilled tradesman. This is an excellent career move, for a number of reasons. For many people, this kind of hands-on, active job is a perfect fit. Construction workers and skilled tradesmen get to move around and work in a variety of different locations; they are never trapped behind a desk watching the hands of a clock! Construction workers and skilled tradesmen get to use a variety of sophisticated tools, which can be a great deal of fun. They can work independently or as part of a team. Also, specialized workers can be highly paid for their services, and can receive excellent career benefits.

Despite all of the physical and financial rewards of a career in construction and the skilled trades, many individuals find that meeting the mental challenges of the job is more satisfying. Construction workers and skilled tradesmen are constantly required to solve problems both great and small. In order to end up with a finished product that looks polished and perfect, a huge number of calculations and adjustments may be made. For this reason, a construction worker or skilled tradesman needs to be adept at considering the various aspects of a problem and imagining realistic and viable solutions. Sometimes the options available to the worker will be limited by resources. When this is the case, a construction worker or skilled tradesman has to be creative in improvising a solution. So, despite outward appearances, the work of a construction worker or skilled tradesman is as much mental as physical.

Another great thing about construction and the skilled trades is the variety of occupations in this field. There are a number of jobs that fall under the umbrella heading of construction and the skilled trades. Here are just a few: carpenter; sheet metal worker; plumber; roofer; welder; pipefitter; painter; concrete mason; brick layer; glazier; millwright; electrical repairman; and heating and air conditioning technician. As you can see, this is a wide range of tasks. All of these jobs, however, require the same basic skills. In order to succeed in construction and the skilled trades, you will need to be able to read with understanding, make quick mechanical calculations, solve basic math problems, and perform arithmetical calculations.

The Construction and Skilled Trades (CAST) examination is designed to measure your knowledge and skill in these areas. This exam is primarily taken as part of the application process for employment at a large construction or service concern. However, a high score on the CAST exam can also be a great way to bolster your resume as an independent contractor. Success on the CAST exam indicates that you have the knowledge and skills required to tackle a multitude of problems. Also, it indicates that you are serious about making a career in this field.

Unfortunately, many would-be construction workers or skilled tradesmen miss out on a great career because they are intimidated by the idea of sitting for a written examination. Many people associate standardized tests with their time in school, and want to avoid the experience any way they can. It is true that some of the topics covered on the CAST exam are similar to those found on more academic tests, like the SAT. However, the material on the CAST is specially adapted to be relevant to individuals interested in construction and the skilled trades. Furthermore, in the mechanical concepts and graphic arithmetic sections of the exam, the CAST focuses exclusively on problems that are likely to be encountered in the course of employment as a construction worker or skilled tradesman. Many test takers find that they actually enjoy solving these problems; after all, it is this pleasure in making and executing plans that has led them to construction in the first place.

In any case, there is no reason why you should not succeed on the CAST exam. With the right kind of preparation, you can ensure a great score. This guidebook has been written as a comprehensive primer to the CAST exam. It contains detailed information about the content and types of questions you will encounter on examination day. After you have spent some time reading this book and practicing the kinds of exercises to be found on the exam, you should have no problem achieving an excellent score!

Test Format

The Construction and Skilled Trades exam is divided into four components: reading comprehension, mechanical concepts, mathematical usage, and graphic arithmetic. You will be required to complete these sections of the exam one at a time, and you will not be allowed to return to previous sections of the exam once they are complete. The reading comprehension section of the exam consists of 32 questions on four long passages of text; these questions must be completed within 30 minutes. The mechanical concepts section of the exam consists of 44 questions which must be answered within 20 minutes. Each of these questions will be based on a depiction of some mechanical problem or situation. The mathematical usage section consists of 18 questions, and must be completed within 7 minutes. These questions require you to solve arithmetic problems and use mathematical formulae. Finally, the graphic arithmetic section of the exam consists of 16 questions, and must be completed within 30 minutes. These questions will be based on two drawings. You will not be allowed to use a calculator on any section of the exam. In all, the CAST exam should take you a little less than two hours to complete. You will be allowed to take short breaks between the sections.

Scoring of the Exam

On the CAST, you will be given an individual score for each of the four sections of the exam. Your four raw scores will be combined to produce an Index Score on a scale from 1 to 10. For all intents and purposes, this Index Score will be the record of your performance on the CAST exam. There is no minimum passing score recommended by the exam administrator; it will be up to your employer to judge your scores. Most scores fall between 3 and 8; both extremely low and extremely high scores are rare. Although the organization that produced the CAST does not make any official statement on the subject, former test administrators have let us know that there is a wrong answer penalty to discourage guessing. What this means for you is that unless you can eliminate two answer choices, guessing is probably not in your best interest.

On the Day of the Exam

When you register for the CAST exam, you will be given detailed information on where and when the examination will be given. The CAST exam is administered at testing facilities around the country; oftentimes, the exam will be administered by a large employer as part of the application process.

No matter where or when you take the exam, there are a few things you can do to maximize your performance. First, and perhaps most importantly, get a good night's sleep before your examination. You do not want to be groggy when you sit for the exam. Also, if you are taking the exam in the morning, be sure to eat a complete and balanced breakfast. Research consistently suggests that jumpstarting the body's metabolism with an early meal increases blood flow to the brain. Being hungry or weak from lack of food can inhibit your ability to concentrate during the exam. If you are taking the exam later in the day, bring a healthy snack (like a banana or a granola bar) to eat right before you begin. Also, be sure to drink plenty of water; like hunger, dehydration can make it difficult to focus your attention. Finally, be sure to wear clothes that are comfortable as well as appropriate for the testing environment. You want to make a good impression on the test administrator, but you also want to wear clothes that will not distract while you work.

How to Use This Book

This book endeavors to be a comprehensive guide to the Construction and Skilled Trades examination. It covers in detail all of the content and question types that will appear on your examination. It may be, however, that you are already fairly knowledgeable in one of the areas covered by the examination. If you are a math expert, for instance, you may already know much of the information covered in the mathematical usage and graphic arithmetic sections. For this reason, do not feel that you have to read this book from cover to cover. Feel free to concentrate your study on those areas of the examination for which you need the most preparation. If you have a limited time to study before the exam, focus your efforts on the content areas that are least familiar to you, as it is in these areas where you'll see the most immediate improvement.

Moreover, you should not try to read this book in its entirety without interruption. A great deal of information has been condensed here, and it would be nearly impossible to retain all of it from a single reading. Here and there, we have indicated practice exercises you can use to supplement the information contained in the book. Practicing the skills described herein is the best way to solidify your knowledge. Also, performing some practice exercises will accustom you to the type of thinking you'll have to do on the exam itself. The best way to use this book in preparation for the CAST exam is to read a little bit at a time for several weeks before the exam. If you can read and practice a small amount every day, you will steadily acquire all of the knowledge and skills you need to ace the exam!

The Mechanical Concepts Test

Transform passive reading into active learning! After immersing yourself in this chapter, put your comprehension to the test by taking a quiz. The insights you gained will stay with you longer this way. Scan the QR code to go directly to the chapter quiz interface for this study guide. If you're using a computer, simply visit the bonus page at **mometrix.com/bonus948/cast** and click the Chapter Quizzes link.

For most CAST test takers, the mechanical concepts section of the exam is the most appealing. People who are interested in plant operation often have an intuitive sense of the physical world, the behavior of machines, and the best ways to accomplish a physical task. All of these areas are covered in the mechanical concepts questions. This section of the exam consists of 44 questions and must be completed within 20 minutes. This may not seem like a great deal of time, but many of the questions will not require more than a few seconds of thought once you have solidified your understanding of the basic concepts of applied physics and mechanics. Each of the 44 questions will be based on a picture and will have three possible answers. The pictures will contain all of the information required to answer the questions. Some of the questions have to do with specific simple machines, while others apply mechanics to more general topics.

In order to succeed on the mechanical concepts section of the CAST exam, you will need to be familiar with basic concepts in physics and mechanics. Don't worry: the CAST exam does not dwell on obscure theories or require you to make complicated calculations. The equations that are included in this section of the book are meant to illustrate the relationships of physics, not to show you how to solve numerical problems. You do, however, need to understand the essential properties of physics and how they apply to real-life situations. In order to help you along, we have included a full primer on all of the concepts that may come up on this section of the exam. Important terms and concepts are placed in bold. Finally, although we have tried to make this section of the guidebook as easy to read as possible, we still recommend that you take your time and avoid reading in a hurry. You may need to read some of this information a few times before fully absorbing it. Whenever possible, try to imagine some everyday examples of the concepts we discuss; after all, applying the theories of physics to the materials of everyday life is one way to define mechanics.

Kinematics

To begin, we will look at the basics of physics. At its heart, physics is just a set of explanations for the ways in which matter and energy behave. There are three key concepts used to describe how matter moves:

1. Displacement
2. Velocity
3. Acceleration

DISPLACEMENT

Concept: Where and how far an object has gone

Calculation: Final position – initial position

When something changes its location from one place to another, it is said to have undergone displacement. If a golf ball is hit across a sloped green into the hole, the displacement only takes into account the final and initial locations, not the path of the ball.

Displacement along a straight line is a very simple example of a vector quantity; it has both a magnitude and a direction. Direction is as important as magnitude in many measurements. If we can determine the original and final position of the object, then we can determine the total displacement with this simple equation:

$$\text{Displacement} = \text{final position} - \text{original position}$$

The hole (final position) is at the Cartesian coordinate location (2,0) and the ball is hit from the location (1,0). The displacement is:

$$\text{Displacement} = (2,0) - (1,0)$$

$$\text{Displacement} = (1,0)$$

The displacement has a magnitude of 1 and a direction of the positive x-direction.

> **Review Video: Displacement in Physics**
> Visit mometrix.com/academy and enter code: 236197

VELOCITY

Concept: The rate of moving from one position to another

Calculation: Change in position / change in time

Velocity answers the question, "How quickly is an object moving?" For example, if a car and a plane travel between two cities that are a hundred miles apart, but the car takes two hours and the plane takes one hour, the car has the same displacement as the plane but a smaller velocity.

In order to solve some of the problems on the exam, you may need to assess the velocity of an object. If we want to calculate the average velocity of an object, we must know two things. First, we must know its displacement. Second, we must know the time it took to cover this distance. The formula for average velocity is quite simple:

$$\text{average velocity} = \frac{\text{displacement}}{\text{change in time}}$$

Or

$$\text{average velocity} = \frac{\text{final position} - \text{original position}}{\text{final time} - \text{original time}}$$

To complete the example, the velocity of the plane is calculated to be:

$$\text{plane average velocity} = \frac{100 \text{ miles}}{1 \text{ hour}} = 100 \text{ miles per hour}$$

The velocity of the car is less:

$$\text{car average velocity} = \frac{100 \text{ miles}}{2 \text{ hours}} = 50 \text{ miles per hour}$$

Often, people confuse the words *speed* and *velocity*. There is a significant difference. The average velocity is based on the amount of displacement, a vector. Alternately, the average speed is based on the distance covered or the path length. The equation for speed is:

$$\text{average speed} = \frac{\text{total distance traveled}}{\text{change in time}}$$

Notice that we used total distance and *not* change in position, because speed is path-dependent.

If the plane traveling between cities had needed to fly around a storm on its way, making the distance traveled 50 miles greater than the distance the car traveled, the plane would still have the same total displacement as the car.

For this reason, the average speed can be calculated:

$$\text{plane average speed} = \frac{150 \text{ miles}}{1 \text{ hour}} = 150 \text{ miles per hour}$$

$$\text{car average speed} = \frac{100 \text{ miles}}{2 \text{ hours}} = 50 \text{ miles per hour}$$

ACCELERATION

Concept: How quickly something changes from one velocity to another

Calculation: Change in velocity / change in time

Acceleration is the rate of change of the velocity of an object. If a car accelerates from zero velocity to 60 miles per hour (88 feet per second) in two seconds, the car has an impressive acceleration. But if a car performs the same change in velocity in eight seconds, the acceleration is much lower and not as impressive.

To calculate average acceleration, we may use the equation:

$$\text{average acceleration} = \frac{\text{change in velocity}}{\text{change in time}}$$

The acceleration of the cars is found to be:

$$\text{Car \#1 average acceleration} = \frac{88 \text{ feet per second}}{2 \text{ seconds}} = 44 \frac{\text{feet}}{\text{second}^2}$$

$$\text{Car \#2 average acceleration} = \frac{88 \text{ feet per second}}{8 \text{ seconds}} = 11 \frac{\text{feet}}{\text{second}^2}$$

Acceleration will be expressed in units of distance divided by time squared; for instance, meters per second squared or feet per second squared.

> **Review Video: Displacement, Velocity, and Acceleration**
> Visit mometrix.com/academy and enter code: 671849
>
> **Review Video: Newton's Law of Gravitation**
> Visit mometrix.com/academy and enter code: 709086

PROJECTILE MOTION

A specific application of the study of motion is projectile motion. Simple projectile motion occurs when an object is in the air and experiencing only the force of gravity. We will disregard drag for this topic. Some common examples of projectile motion are thrown balls, flying bullets, and falling rocks. The characteristics of projectile motion are:

1. The horizontal component of velocity doesn't change
2. The vertical acceleration due to gravity affects the vertical component of velocity

Because gravity only acts downwards, objects in projectile motion only experience acceleration in the y-direction (vertical). The horizontal component of the object's velocity does not change in flight. This means that if a rock is thrown out off a cliff, the horizontal velocity (think of the shadow if the sun is directly overhead) will not change until the ball hits the ground.

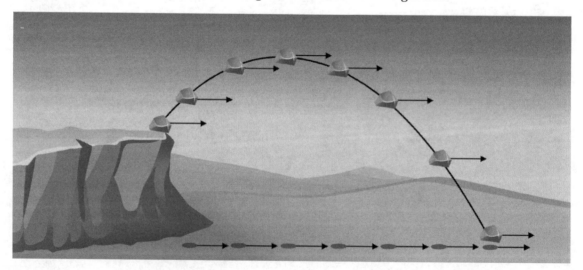

The velocity in the vertical direction is affected by gravity. Gravity imposes an acceleration of $g = 9.8 \frac{m}{s^2}$ or $32 \frac{ft}{s^2}$ downward on projectiles. The vertical component of velocity at any point is equal to:

$$\text{vertical velocity} = \text{original vertical velocity} - g \times \text{time}$$

When these characteristics are combined, there are three points of particular interest in a projectile's flight. At the beginning of a flight, the object has a horizontal component and a vertical component giving it a large speed. At the top of a projectile's flight, the vertical velocity equals zero, making the top the slowest part of travel. When the object passes the same height as the launch, the vertical velocity is opposite of the initial vertical velocity, making the speed equal to the initial speed.

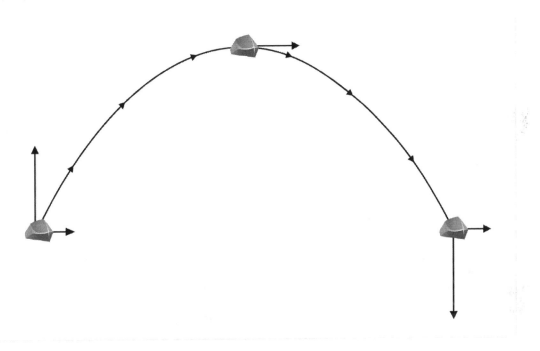

If the object continues falling below the initial height from which it was launched (e.g., it was launched from the edge of a cliff), it will have an even greater velocity than it did initially from that point until it hits the ground.

> **Review Video: Projectile Motion**
> Visit mometrix.com/academy and enter code: 719700

Rotational Kinematics

Concept: Increasing the radius increases the linear speed

Calculation: Linear speed $=$ radius $\times$ rotational speed

Another interesting application of the study of motion is rotation. In practice, simple rotation is when an object rotates around a point at a constant speed. Most questions covering rotational kinematics will provide the distance from a rotating object to the center of rotation (radius) and ask about the linear speed of the object. A point will have a greater linear speed when it is farther from the center of rotation.

If a potter is spinning his wheel at a constant speed of one revolution per second, the clay six inches away from the center will be going faster than the clay three inches from the center. The clay directly in the center of the wheel will not have any linear velocity.

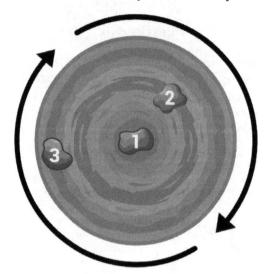

To find the linear speed of rotating objects using radians, we use the equation:

linear speed = (rotational speed [in radians]) × (radius)

Using degrees, the equation is:

$$\textbf{linear speed = (rotational speed [in degrees])} \times \frac{\boldsymbol{\pi} \textbf{ radians}}{\textbf{180 degrees}} \times \textbf{(radius)}$$

To find the speed of the pieces of clay, we use the known values (rotational speed of 1 revolution per second, radii of 0 inches, 3 inches, and 6 inches) and the knowledge that one revolution = 2π.

$$\text{clay \#1 speed} = \left(2\pi \frac{\text{rad}}{\text{s}}\right) \times (0 \text{ inches}) = 0 \frac{\text{inches}}{\text{second}}$$

$$\text{clay \#2 speed} = \left(2\pi \frac{\text{rad}}{\text{s}}\right) \times (3 \text{ inches}) = 18.8 \frac{\text{inches}}{\text{second}}$$

$$\text{clay \#3 speed} = \left(2\pi \frac{\text{rad}}{\text{s}}\right) \times (6 \text{ inches}) = 37.7 \frac{\text{inches}}{\text{second}}$$

> **Review Video: <u>Linear Speed</u>**
> Visit mometrix.com/academy and enter code: 327101

CAMS

In the study of motion, a final application often tested is the cam. A cam and follower system allows mechanical systems to have timed, specified, and repeating motion. Although cams come in varied forms, tests focus on rotary cams. In engines, a cam shaft coordinates the valves for intake and exhaust. Cams are often used to convert rotational motion into repeating linear motion.

Cams rotate around one point. The follower sits on the edge of the cam and moves along with the edge. To understand simple cams, count the number of bumps on the cam. Each bump will cause the follower to move outwards.

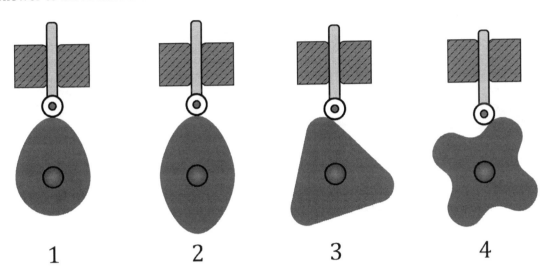

Another way to consider cams is to unravel the cam profile into a straight object. The follower will then follow the top of the profile.

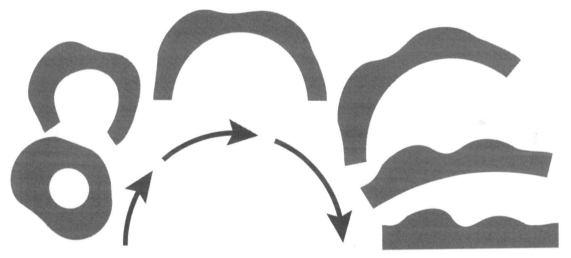

Kinetics

NEWTON'S THREE LAWS OF MECHANICS

The questions on the exam may require you to demonstrate familiarity with the concepts expressed in Newton's three laws of motion which relate to the concept of force.

Newton's first law – A body at rest tends to remain at rest, while a body in motion tends to remain in motion, unless acted upon by an external force.

Newton's second law – The acceleration of an object is directly proportional to the force being exerted on it and inversely proportional to its mass.

Newton's third law – For every force, there is an equal and opposite force.

FIRST LAW

Concept: Unless something interferes, an object won't start or stop moving

Although intuition supports the idea that objects do not start moving until a force acts on them, the idea of an object continuing forever without any forces can seem odd. Before Newton formulated his laws of mechanics, general thought held that some force had to act on an object continuously in order for it to move at a constant velocity. This seems to make sense; when an object is briefly pushed, it will eventually come to a stop. Newton, however, determined that unless some other force acted on the object (most notably friction or air resistance), it would continue in the direction it was pushed at the same velocity forever.

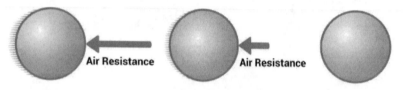

As time moves forward, the air resistance stops one ball, but the ball without air resistance has no stopping force.

> **Review Video: Newton's First Law of Motion**
> Visit mometrix.com/academy and enter code: 590367

SECOND LAW

Concept: Acceleration increases linearly with force.

Although Newton's second law can be conceptually understood as a series of relationships describing how an increase in one factor will decrease another factor, the law can be understood best in equation format:

$$\text{Force} = \text{mass} \times \text{acceleration}$$

Or

$$\text{Acceleration} = \frac{\text{force}}{\text{mass}}$$

Or

$$\text{Mass} = \frac{\text{force}}{\text{acceleration}}$$

Each of the forms of this equation allows for a different look at the same relationships. To examine the relationships, change one factor and observe the result. If a steel ball with a diameter of 6.3 cm has a mass of 1 kg and an acceleration of 1 m/s², then the net force on the ball will be 1 Newton.

Review Video: <u>Newton's Second Law of Motion</u>
Visit mometrix.com/academy and enter code: 737975

THIRD LAW

Concept: Nothing can push or pull without being pushed or pulled in return.

When any object exerts a force on another object, the other object exerts the opposite force back on the original object. To observe this, consider two spring-based fruit scales, both tipped on their sides as shown with the weighing surfaces facing each other. If fruit scale #1 is pressing fruit scale #2 into the wall, it exerts a force on fruit scale #2, measurable by the reading on scale #2. However, because fruit scale #1 is exerting a force on scale #2, scale #2 is exerting a force on scale #1 with an opposite direction, but the same magnitude.

Review Video: <u>Newton's Third Law of Motion</u>
Visit mometrix.com/academy and enter code: 838401

FORCE

Concept: A push or pull on an object

Calculation: Force = mass × acceleration

A force is a vector that causes acceleration of a body. Force has both magnitude and direction. Furthermore, multiple forces acting on one object combine in vector addition. This can be demonstrated by considering an object placed at the origin of the coordinate plane. If it is pushed along the positive direction of the x-axis, it will move in this direction. If the force acting on it is in the positive direction of the y-axis, it will move in that direction.

However, if both forces are applied at the same time, then the object will move at an angle to both the x- and y-axes, an angle determined by the relative amount of force exerted in each direction. In this way, we may see that the resulting force is a vector sum; a net force that has both magnitude and direction.

Resultant vectors from applied forces:

> **Review Video: Push and Pull Forces**
> Visit mometrix.com/academy and enter code: 104731

MASS

Concept: The amount of matter

Mass can be defined as the quantity of matter in an object. If we apply the same force to two objects of different mass, we will find that the resulting acceleration is different. In other words, the acceleration of an object is directly proportional to the force being exerted on it and inversely proportional to its mass.

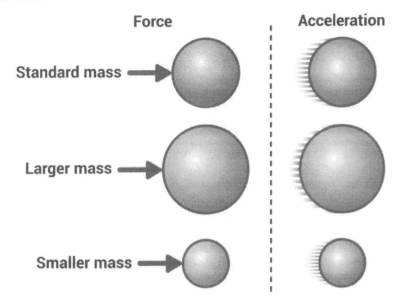

GRAVITY

Gravity is a force that exists between all objects with matter. Gravity is a pulling force between objects, meaning that the forces on the objects point toward the opposite object. When Newton's third law is applied to gravity, the force pairs from gravity are shown to be equal in magnitude and opposite in direction.

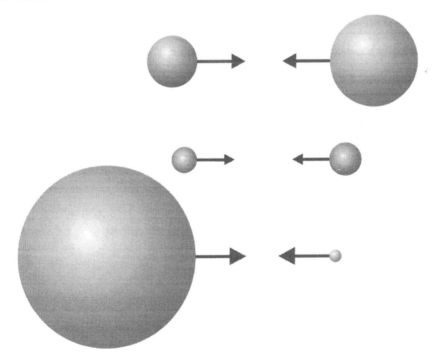

WEIGHT

Weight is sometimes confused with mass. While mass is the amount of matter, weight is the force exerted by the earth on an object with matter by gravity. The earth pulls every object of mass toward its center while every object of mass pulls the earth toward its center. The object's pull on the earth is equal in magnitude to the pull which the earth exerts, but, because the mass of the earth is very large in comparison (5.97×10^{24} kg), only the object appears to be affected by the force.

The gravity of the earth causes a constant acceleration due to gravity (g) at a specific altitude. For most earthbound applications, the acceleration due to gravity is 32.2 ft/s^2 or 9.8 m/s^2 in a downward direction. The equation for the force of gravity (weight) on an object is the equation from Newton's Second Law with the constant acceleration due to gravity (g).

$$\textbf{Weight} = \textbf{mass} \times \textbf{acceleration due to gravity}$$

$$\mathbf{W = m \times g}$$

The SI (International Standard of Units) unit for weight is the Newton $\left(\frac{\text{kg} \times \text{m}}{\text{s}^2}\right)$. The English Engineering unit system uses the pound, or lb, as the unit for weight and force $\left(\frac{\text{slug} \times \text{ft}}{\text{s}^2}\right)$. Thus, a 2 kg object under the influence of gravity would have a weight of:

$$W = 2 \text{ kg} \times 9.8 \frac{\text{m}}{\text{s}^2} = 19.6 \text{ N downward}$$

> **Review Video: Mass, Weight, Volume, Density, and Specific Gravity**
> Visit mometrix.com/academy and enter code: 920570

NORMAL FORCE

Concept: The force perpendicular to a contact surface

The word *normal* is used in mathematics to mean perpendicular, and so the force known as normal force should be remembered as the perpendicular force exerted on an object that is resting on some other surface. For instance, if a box is resting on a horizontal surface, we may say that the normal force is directed upwards through the box (the opposite, downward force is the weight of the box).

If the box is resting on a wedge, the normal force from the wedge is not vertical but is perpendicular to the wedge edge.

TENSION

Concept: A pulling force like that from a cord or rope.

Another force that may come into play on the exam is called tension. Anytime a cord is attached to a body and pulled so that it is taut, we may say that the cord is under tension. The cord in tension applies a pulling tension force on the connected objects. This force is pointed away from the body and along the cord at the point of attachment. In simple considerations of tension, the cord is assumed to be both without mass and incapable of stretching. In other words, its only role is as the connector between two bodies. The cord is also assumed to pull on both ends with the same magnitude of tension force.

FRICTION

Concept: Friction is a resistance to motion between contacting surfaces

In order to illustrate the concept of friction, let us imagine a book resting on a table. As it sits, the force of its weight is equal to and opposite of the normal force. If, however, we were to exert a force on the book, attempting to push it to one side, a frictional force would arise, equal and opposite to our force. This kind of frictional force is known as static frictional force.

As we increase our force on the book, however, we will eventually cause it to accelerate in the direction of our force. At this point, the frictional force opposing us will be known as kinetic friction. For many combinations of surfaces, the magnitude of the kinetic frictional force is lower than that of the static frictional force, and consequently, the amount of force needed to maintain the movement of the book will be less than that needed to initiate the movement.

Review Video: Friction
Visit mometrix.com/academy and enter code: 716782

ROLLING FRICTION

Occasionally, a question will ask you to consider the amount of friction generated by an object that is rolling. If a wheel is rolling at a constant speed, then the point at which it touches the ground will not slide, and there will be no friction between the ground and the wheel inhibiting movement. In fact, the friction at the point of contact between the wheel and the ground is static friction necessary to propel with wheels. When a vehicle accelerates, the static friction between the wheels and the ground allows the vehicle to achieve acceleration. Without this friction, the vehicle would spin its wheels and go nowhere.

Although the static friction does not impede movement for the wheels, a combination of frictional forces can resist rolling motion. One such frictional force is bearing friction. Bearing friction is the kinetic friction between the wheel and an object it rotates around, such as a stationary axle.

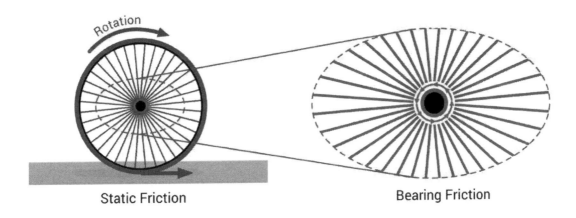

Static Friction   Bearing Friction

DRAG FORCE

Friction can also be generated when an object is moving through air or liquid. A drag force occurs when a body moves through some fluid (either liquid or gas) and experiences a force that opposes the motion of the body. The drag force is greater if the air or fluid is thicker or is moving in the direction opposite to the object. Obviously, the higher the drag force, the greater amount of positive force required to keep the object moving forward.

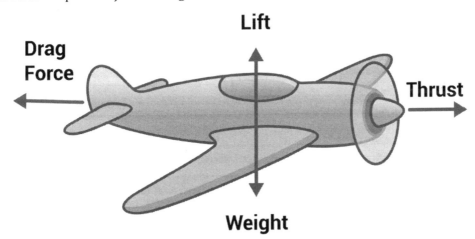

BALANCED FORCES

An object is in equilibrium when the sum of all forces acting on the object is zero. When the forces on an object sum to zero, the object does not accelerate. Equilibrium can be obtained when forces in the y-direction sum to zero, forces in the x-direction sum to zero, or forces in both directions sum to zero.

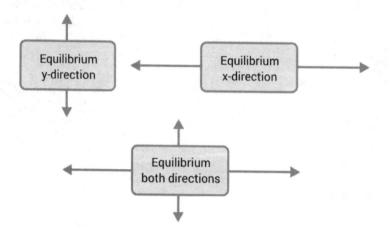

In most cases, a problem will provide one or more forces acting on an object and ask for a force to balance the system. The force will be the opposite of the current force or sum of current forces.

Balance the forces

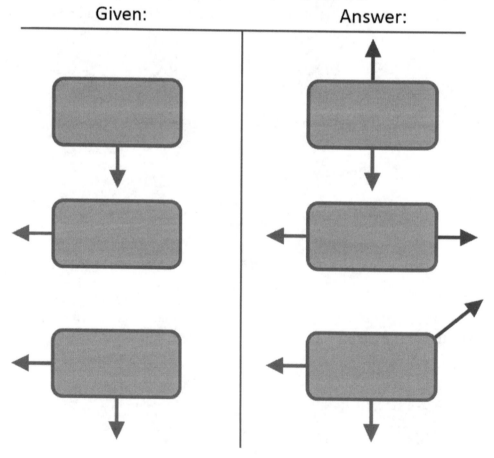

ROTATIONAL KINETICS

Many equations and concepts in linear kinematics and kinetics transfer to rotation. For example, angular position is an angle. Angular velocity, like linear velocity, is the change in the position (angle) divided by the time. Angular acceleration is the change in angular velocity divided by time. Although most tests will not require you to perform angular calculations, they will expect you to understand the angular version of force: torque.

Concept: Torque is a twisting force on an object

Calculation: Torque = radius × force

Torque, like force, is a vector and has magnitude and direction. As with force, the sum of torques on an object will affect the angular acceleration of that object. The key to solving problems with torque is understanding the lever arm. A better description of the torque equation is:

Torque = force × the distance perpedicular to the force from the center of rotation

Because torque is directly proportional to the radius, or lever arm, a greater lever arm will result in a greater torque with the same amount of force. The wrench on the right has twice the radius and, as a result, twice the torque.

Alternatively, a greater force also increases torque. The wrench on the right has twice the force and twice the torque.

Work/Energy

WORK

Concept: Work is the transfer of energy from one object to another

Calculation: Work = force × displacement

The equation for work in one dimension is fairly simple: $W = F \times d$ In the equation, the force and the displacement are the magnitude of the force exerted and the total change in position of the object on which the force is exerted, respectively. If force and displacement have the same direction, then the work is positive. If they are in opposite directions, however, the work is negative.

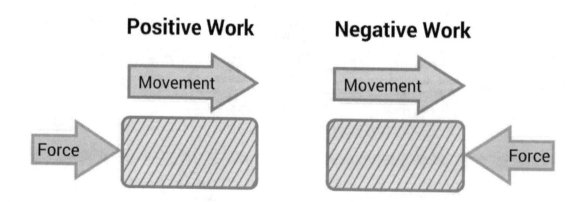

For two-dimensional work, the equation is a bit more complex:

Work = Force × displacement × cos(θ between displacement and force)

$$W = F \times d \times \cos(\theta)$$

The angle in the equation is the angle between the direction of the force and the direction of the displacement. Thus, the work done when a box is pulled at a 20 degree angle with a force of 100 lb

36

for 20 ft will be less than the work done when a differently weighted box is pulled horizontally with a force of 100 lb for 20 ft.

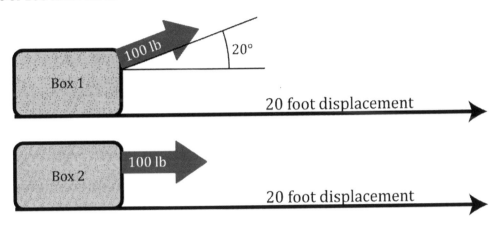

$$W_1 = 100\text{lb} \times 20\text{ft} \times \cos(20°) = 1880 \text{ ft} \cdot \text{lb}$$

$$W_2 = 100\text{lb} \times 20\text{ft} \times \cos(0°) = 2000 \text{ ft} \cdot \text{lb}$$

The unit ft · lb is the unit for both work and energy.

Review Video: Work
Visit mometrix.com/academy and enter code: 681834

ENERGY

Concept: The ability of a body to do work on another object

Energy is a word that has developed several different meanings in the English language, but in physics, it refers to the measure of a body's ability to do work. In physics, energy may not have a million meanings, but it does have many forms. Each of these forms, such as chemical, electric, and nuclear, is the capability of an object to perform work. However, for the purpose of most tests, mechanical energy and mechanical work are the only forms of energy worth understanding in depth. Mechanical energy is the sum of an object's kinetic and potential energies. Although they will be introduced in greater detail, these are the forms of mechanical energy:

Kinetic Energy – energy an object has by virtue of its motion

Gravitational Potential Energy – energy by virtue of an object's height

Elastic Potential Energy – energy stored in compression or tension

Neglecting frictional forces, mechanical energy is conserved.

As an example, imagine a ball moving perpendicular to the surface of the earth, in other words straight up and down, with its weight being the only force acting on it. As the ball rises, the weight will be doing work on the ball, decreasing its speed and its kinetic energy and slowing it down until it momentarily stops. During this ascent, the potential energy of the ball will be rising. Once the ball begins to fall back down, it will lose potential energy as it gains kinetic energy. Mechanical energy is conserved throughout; the potential energy of the ball at its highest point is equal to the kinetic energy of the ball at its lowest point prior to impact.

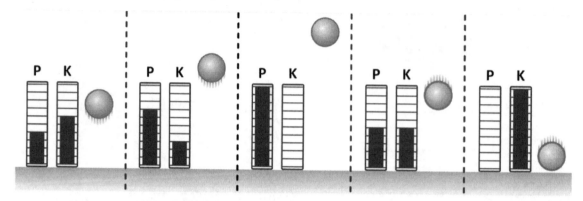

In systems where friction and air resistance are not negligible, we observe a different sort of result. For example, imagine a block sliding across the floor until it comes to a stop due to friction. Unlike a compressed spring or a ball flung into the air, there is no way for this block to regain its energy with a return trip. Therefore, we cannot say that the lost kinetic energy is being stored as potential energy. Instead, it has been dissipated and cannot be recovered. The total mechanical energy of the block-floor system has been not conserved in this case but rather reduced. The total energy of the system has not decreased, since the kinetic energy has been converted into thermal energy, but that energy is no longer useful for work.

Energy, though it may change form, will be neither created nor destroyed during physical processes. However, if we construct a system and some external force performs work on it, the result may be slightly different. If the work is positive, then the overall store of energy is increased; if it is negative, however, we can say that the overall energy of the system has decreased.

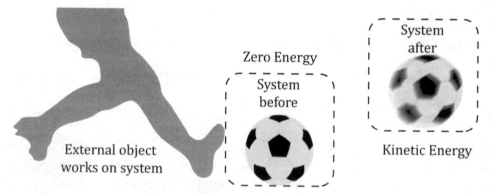

KINETIC ENERGY

The kinetic energy of an object is the amount of energy it possesses by reason of being in motion. Kinetic energy cannot be negative. Changes in kinetic energy will occur when a force does work on an object, such that the motion of the object is altered. This change in kinetic energy is equal to the amount of work that is done. This relationship is commonly referred to as the work-energy theorem.

One interesting application of the work-energy theorem is that of objects in a free fall. To begin with, let us assert that the force acting on such an object is its weight, which is equal to its mass times g (the force of gravity). The work done by this force will be positive, as the force is exerted in the direction in which the object is traveling. Kinetic energy will, therefore, increase, according to the work-kinetic energy theorem.

If the object is dropped from a great enough height, it eventually reaches its terminal velocity, where the drag force is equal to the weight, so the object is no longer accelerating and its kinetic energy remains constant.

GRAVITATIONAL POTENTIAL ENERGY

Gravitational potential energy is simply the potential for a certain amount of work to be done by one object on another using gravity. For objects on earth, the gravitational potential energy is equal to the amount of work which the earth can act on the object. The work which gravity performs on objects moving entirely or partially in the vertical direction is equal to the force exerted by the earth (weight) times the distance traveled in the direction of the force (height above the ground or reference point): Work from gravity = weight × height above the ground. Thus, the gravitational potential energy is the same as the potential work.

Gravitational Potential Energy = weight × height

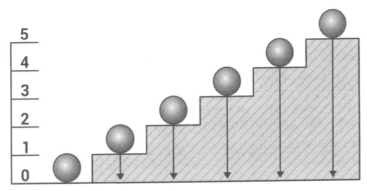

ELASTIC POTENTIAL ENERGY

Elastic potential energy is the potential for a certain amount of work to be done by one object on another using elastic compression or tension. The most common example is the spring. A spring will resist any compression or tension away from its equilibrium position (natural position). A small buggy is pressed into a large spring. The spring contains a large amount of elastic potential energy. If the buggy and spring are released, the spring will exert a force on the buggy, pushing it for a distance. This work will put kinetic energy into the buggy. The energy can be imagined as a liquid poured from one container into another. The spring pours its elastic energy into the buggy, which receives the energy as kinetic energy.

Review Video: Potential and Kinetic Energy
Visit mometrix.com/academy and enter code: 491502

POWER

Concept: The rate of work

Calculation: Work/time

On occasion, you may need to demonstrate an understanding of power as it is defined in applied physics. Power is the rate at which work is done. Power, like work and energy, is a scalar quantity. Power can be calculated by dividing the amount of work performed by the amount of time in which the work was performed: **Power** $= \frac{\text{work}}{\text{time}}$. If more work is performed in a shorter amount of time, more power has been exerted. Power can be expressed in a variety of units. The preferred metric expression is one of watts or joules per seconds. Engine power is often expressed in horsepower.

Machines

SIMPLE MACHINES
Concept: Tools which transform forces to make tasks easier.

As their job is to transform forces, simple machines have an input force and an output force or forces. Simple machines transform forces in two ways: direction and magnitude. A machine can change the direction of a force, with respect to the input force, like a single stationary pulley which only changes the direction of the output force. A machine can also change the magnitude of the force like a lever.

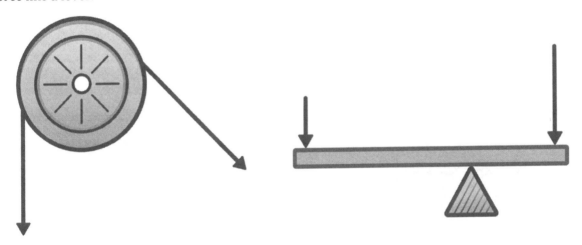

Simple machines include the inclined plane, the wedge, the screw, the pulley, the lever, and the wheel.

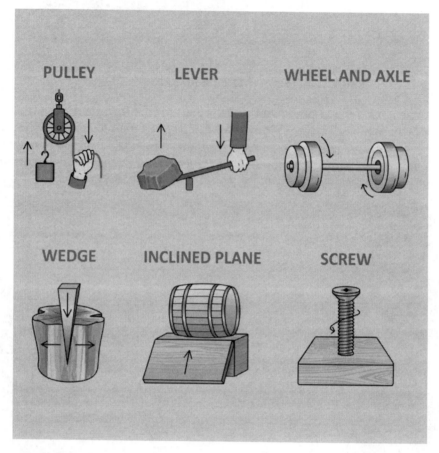

MECHANICAL ADVANTAGE

Concept: The amount of change a simple machine provides to the magnitude of a force

Calculation: Output force/input force

Mechanical advantage is the measure of the output force divided by the input force. Thus, mechanical advantage measures the change performed by a machine. Machines cannot create energy, only transform it. Thus, in frictionless, ideal machines, the input work equals the output work.

$$\text{Work}_{\text{input}} = \text{Work}_{\text{output}}$$

$$\text{force}_{\text{input}} \times \text{distance}_{\text{input}} = \text{force}_{\text{output}} \times \text{distance}_{\text{output}}$$

This means that a simple machine can increase the force of the output by decreasing the distance which the output travels or it can increase the distance of the output by decreasing the force at the output.

By moving parts of the equation for work, we can arrive at the equation for mechanical advantage.

$$\text{Mechanical Advantage} = \frac{\text{force}_{\text{output}}}{\text{force}_{\text{input}}} = \frac{\text{distance}_{\text{input}}}{\text{distance}_{\text{output}}}$$

42

If the mechanical advantage is greater than one, the output force is greater than the input force and the input distance is greater than the output distance. Conversely, if the mechanical advantage is less than one, the input force is greater than the output force and the output distance is greater than the input distance. In equation form this is:

If Mechanical Advantage > 1:

$$\text{force}_{\text{input}} < \text{force}_{\text{output}} \text{ and distance}_{\text{output}} < \text{distance}_{\text{input}}$$

If Mechanical Advantage < 1:

$$\text{force}_{\text{input}} > \text{force}_{\text{output}} \text{ and distance}_{\text{output}} > \text{distance}_{\text{input}}$$

INCLINED PLANE

The inclined plane is perhaps the most common of the simple machines. It is simply a flat surface that elevates as you move from one end to the other; a ramp is an easy example of an inclined plane. Consider how much easier it is for an elderly person to walk up a long ramp than to climb a shorter but steeper flight of stairs; this is because the force required is diminished as the distance increases. Indeed, the longer the ramp, the easier it is to ascend.

On the exam, this simple fact will most often be applied to moving heavy objects. For instance, if you have to move a heavy box onto the back of a truck, it is much easier to push it up a ramp than to lift it directly onto the truck bed. The longer the ramp, the greater the mechanical advantage, and the easier it will be to move the box. The mechanical advantage of an inclined plane is equal to the slant length divided by the rise of the plane.

$$\text{Mechanical Advantage} = \frac{\text{slant length}}{\text{rise}}$$

As you solve this kind of problem, however, remember that the same amount of work is being performed whether the box is lifted directly or pushed up a twenty-foot ramp; a simple machine only changes the force and the distance.

WEDGE

A wedge is a variation on the inclined plane, in which the wedge moves between objects or parts and forces them apart. The unique characteristic of a wedge is that, unlike an inclined plane, it is designed to move. Perhaps the most familiar use of the wedge is in splitting wood. A wedge is driven into the wood by hitting the flat back end. The thin end of a wedge is easier to drive into the wood since it has less surface area and, therefore, transmits more force per area. As the wedge is driven in, the increased width helps to split the wood.

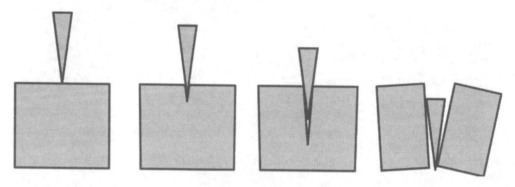

The exam may require you to select the wedge that has the highest mechanical advantage. This should be easy: the longer and thinner the wedge, the greater the mechanical advantage. The equation for mechanical advantage is:

$$\text{Mechanical Advantage} = \frac{\textbf{Length}}{\textbf{Width}}$$

SCREW

A screw is simply an inclined plane that has been wound around a cylinder so that it forms a sort of spiral.

When it is placed into some medium, as for instance wood, the screw will move either forward or backward when it is rotated. The principle of the screw is used in a number of different objects, from jar lids to flashlights. On the exam, you are unlikely to see many questions regarding screws, though you may be presented with a given screw rotation and asked in which direction the screw will move. However, for consistency's sake, the equation for the mechanical advantage is a modification of the inclined plane's equation. Again, the formula for an inclined plane is:

$$\text{Mechanical Advantage} = \frac{\textbf{slant length}}{\textbf{rise}}$$

Because the rise of the inclined plane is the length along a screw, length between rotations = rise. Also, the slant length will equal the circumference of one rotation = 2πr.

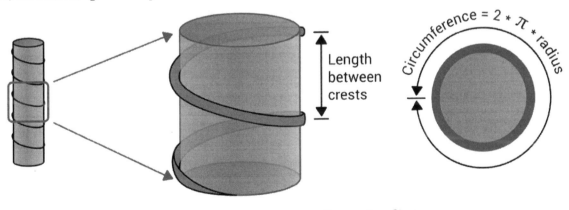

$$\text{Mechanical Advantage} = \frac{\textbf{2} \times \boldsymbol{\pi} \times \textbf{radius}}{\textbf{length between crests}}$$

LEVER

The lever is the most common kind of simple machine. See-saws, shovels, and baseball bats are all examples of levers. There are three classes of levers which are differentiated by the relative orientations of the fulcrum, resistance, and effort. The fulcrum is the point at which the lever rotates, the effort is the point on the lever where force is applied, and the resistance is the part of the lever that acts in response to the effort.

The mechanical advantage of a lever depends on the distances of the effort and resistance from the fulcrum.

$$\text{Mechanical Advantage} = \frac{\text{effort distance}}{\text{resistance distance}}$$

Each class of lever has a different arrangement of effort, fulcrum, and resistance:

First-Class Lever

First-Class Lever

Second-Class Lever

Second-Class Lever

Third-Class Lever

Third-Class Lever

Resistance distance

Resistance

Effort distance

Effort

Fulcrum

In a first-class lever, the fulcrum is between the effort and the resistance. A seesaw is a good example of a first-class lever when effort is applied to force one end up, the other end goes down, and vice versa. The shorter the distance between the fulcrum and the resistance, the easier it will be to move the resistance. As an example, consider whether it is easier to lift another person on a see-saw when they are sitting close to the middle or all the way at the end. A little practice will show you that it is much more difficult to lift a person the farther away he or she is on the see-saw.

In a second-class lever, the resistance is in between the fulcrum and the effort. While a first-class lever is able to increase force and distance through mechanical advantage, a second-class lever is only able to increase force. A common example of a second-class lever is the wheelbarrow; the force exerted by your hand at one end of the wheelbarrow is magnified at the load. Basically, with a second-class lever, you are trading distance for force; by moving your end of the wheelbarrow a bit farther, you produce greater force at the load.

Third-class levers are used to produce greater distance. In a third-class lever, the force is applied in between the fulcrum and the resistance. A baseball bat is a classic example of a third-class lever; the bottom of the bat, below where you grip it, is considered the fulcrum. The end of the bat, where the ball is struck, is the resistance. By exerting effort at the base of the bat, close to the fulcrum, you are able to make the end of the bat fly quickly through the air. The closer your hands are to the base of the bat, the faster you will be able to make the other end of the bat travel.

PULLEY

The pulley is a simple machine in which a rope is carried by the rotation of a wheel. Another name for a pulley is a block. Pulleys are typically used to allow the force to be directed from a convenient location. For instance, imagine you are given the task of lifting a heavy and tall bookcase. Rather than tying a rope to the bookcase and trying to lift it, it would make sense to tie a pulley system to a rafter above the bookcase and run the rope through it, so that you could pull down on the rope and lift the bookcase. Pulling down allows you to incorporate your weight (normal force) into the act of lifting, thereby making it easier.

If there is just one pulley above the bookcase, you have created a first-class lever that will not diminish the amount of force that needs to be applied to lift the bookcase. There is another way to use a pulley, however, that can make the job of lifting a heavy object considerably easier. First, tie the rope directly to the rafter. Then, attach a pulley to the top of the bookcase and run the rope through it. If you can then stand so that you are above the bookcase, you will have a much easier time lifting this heavy object. Why? Because the weight of the bookcase is now being distributed: half of it is acting on the rafter, and half of it is acting on you. In other words, this arrangement allows you to lift an object with half the force. This simple pulley system, therefore, has a mechanical advantage of 2. Note that in this arrangement, the unfixed pulley is acting like a second-class lever. The price you pay for your mechanical advantage is that whatever distance you raise your end of the rope, the bookcase will only be lifted half as much.

Of course, it might be difficult for you to find a place high enough to enact this system. If this is the case, you can always tie another pulley to the rafter and run the rope through it and back down to the floor. Since this second pulley is fixed, the mechanical advantage will remain the same.

There are other, slightly more complex ways to obtain an even greater mechanical advantage with a system of pulleys. On the exam, you may be required to determine the pulley and tackle (rope) arrangement that creates the greatest mechanical advantage. The easiest way to determine the answer is to count the number of ropes that are going to and from the unfixed pulley; the more ropes coming and going, the greater the mechanical advantage.

WHEEL AND AXLE

Another basic arrangement that makes use of simple machines is called the wheel and axle. When most people think of a wheel and axle, they immediately envision an automobile tire. The steering wheel of the car, however, operates on the same mechanical principle, namely that the force required to move the center of a circle is much greater than the force required to move the outer rim of a circle. When you turn the steering wheel, you are essentially using a second-class lever by increasing the output force by increasing the input distance. The force required to turn the wheel from the outer rim is much less than would be required to turn the wheel from its center. Just imagine how difficult it would be to drive a car if the steering wheel was the size of a saucer!

Conceptually, the mechanical advantage of a wheel is easy to understand. For instance, all other things being equal, the mechanical advantage created by a system will increase along with the radius. In other words, a steering wheel with a radius of 12 inches has a greater mechanical advantage than a steering wheel with a radius of ten inches; the same amount of force exerted on the rim of each wheel will produce greater force at the axis of the larger wheel.

> **Review Video: Simple Machines – Wheel and Axle**
> Visit mometrix.com/academy and enter code: 574045

The equation for the mechanical advantage of a wheel and axle is:

$$\text{Mechanical Advantage} = \frac{\text{radius}_{\text{wheel}}}{\text{radius}_{\text{axle}}}$$

Thus, the mechanical advantage of the steering wheel with a larger radius will be:

$$\text{Mechanical Advantage} = \frac{12 \text{ inches}}{2 \text{ inches}} = 6$$

GEARS

The exam may ask you questions involving some slightly more complex mechanisms. It is very common, for instance, for there to be a couple of questions concerning gears. Gears are a system of interlocking wheels that can create immense mechanical advantages. The amount of mechanical advantage, however, will depend on the gear ratio; that is, on the relation in size between the gears.

When a small gear is driving a big gear, the speed of the big gear is relatively slow; when a big gear is driving a small gear, the speed of the small gear is relatively fast.

The equation for the mechanical advantage is:

$$\textbf{Mechanical Advantage} = \frac{\textbf{Torque}_{\textbf{output}}}{\textbf{Torque}_{\textbf{input}}} = \frac{r_{\textbf{output}}}{r_{\textbf{input}}} = \frac{\textbf{\# of teeth}_{\textbf{output}}}{\textbf{\# of teeth}_{\textbf{input}}}$$

Note that mechanical advantage is greater than 1 when the output gear is larger. In these cases, the output velocity (ω) will be lower. The equation for the relative speed of a gear system is:

$$\frac{\omega_{\text{input}}}{\omega_{\text{output}}} = \frac{r_{\text{output}}}{r_{\text{input}}}$$

$$Mechanical\ Advantage = \frac{teeth_{output}}{teeth_{input}} = \frac{20}{10} = 2$$

$$Mechanical\ Advantage = \frac{teeth_{output}}{teeth_{input}} = \frac{16}{8} = 2$$

USES OF GEARS

Gears are used to change the direction, location, and amount of output torque, as well as change the angular velocity of output.

Change output direction

Change torque location

Change torque amount

Change output velocity

GEAR RATIOS

A gear ratio is a measure of how much the speed and torque are changing in a gear system. It is the ratio of output speed to input speed. Because the number of teeth is directly proportional to the speed in meshing gears, a gear ratio can also be calculated using the number of teeth on the gears. When the driving gear has 30 teeth and the driven gear has 10 teeth, the gear ratio is 3:1.

$$\text{Gear Ratio} = \frac{\text{\# of teeth}_{driving}}{\text{\# of teeth}_{driven}} = \frac{30}{10} = \frac{3}{1} = 3:1$$

This means that the smaller, driven gear rotates 3 times for every 1 rotation of the driving gear.

THE HYDRAULIC JACK

The hydraulic jack is a simple machine using two tanks and two pistons to change the amount of an output force.

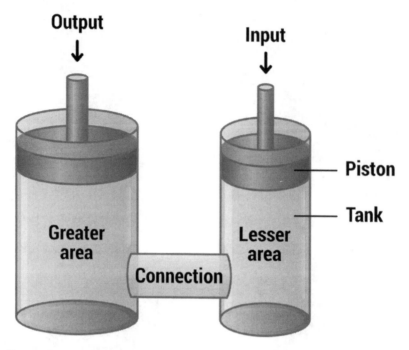

Since fluids are effectively incompressible, when you apply pressure to one part of a contained fluid, that pressure will have to be relieved in equal measure elsewhere in the container. Suppose the input piston has half the surface area of the output piston (10 in^2 compared to 20 in^2), and it is being pushed downward with 50 pounds of force. The pressure being applied to the fluid is $50 \text{ lb} \div 10 \text{ in}^2 = 5 \frac{\text{lb}}{\text{in}^2}$ or 5 psi. When that 5 psi of pressure is applied to the output piston, it pushes that piston upward with a force of $5 \frac{\text{lb}}{\text{in}^2} \times 20 \text{ in}^2 = 100 \text{ lb}$.

The hydraulic jack functions similarly to a first-class lever, but with the important factor being the area of the pistons rather than the length of the lever arms. Note that the mechanical advantage is based on the relative areas, not the relative radii, of the pistons. The radii must be squared to compute the relative areas.

$$\text{Mechanical Advantage} = \frac{\text{Force}_{\text{output}}}{\text{Force}_{\text{input}}} = \frac{\text{area}_{\text{output}}}{\text{area}_{\text{input}}} = \frac{\text{radius}_{\text{output}}^2}{\text{radius}_{\text{input}}^2}$$

PULLEYS AND BELTS

Another system involves two pulleys connected by a drive belt (a looped band that goes around both pulleys). The operation of this system is similar to that of gears, with the exception that the pulleys will rotate in the same direction, while interlocking gears will rotate in opposite directions.

A smaller pulley will always spin faster than a larger pulley, though the larger pulley will generate more torque.

The speed ratio between the pulleys can be determined by comparing their radii; for instance, a 4-inch pulley and a 12-inch pulley will have a speed ratio of 3:1.

Momentum/Impulse

LINEAR MOMENTUM

Concept: How much a body will resist stopping

Calculation: Momentum = mass × velocity

In physics, linear momentum can be found by multiplying the mass and velocity of an object. Momentum and velocity will always be in the same direction. Newton's second law describes momentum, stating that the rate of change of momentum is proportional to the force exerted and is in the direction of the force. If we assume a closed and isolated system (one in which no objects leave or enter, and upon which the sum of external forces is zero), then we can assume that the momentum of the system will neither increase nor decrease. That is, we will find that the momentum is a constant. The law of conservation of linear momentum applies universally in physics, even in situations of extremely high velocity or with subatomic particles.

COLLISIONS

This concept of momentum takes on new importance when we consider collisions. A collision is an isolated event in which a strong force acts between each of two or more colliding bodies for a brief period of time. However, a collision is more intuitively defined as one or more objects hitting each other.

When two bodies collide, each object exerts a force on the opposite member. These equal and opposite forces change the linear momentum of the objects. However, when both bodies are considered, the net momentum in collisions is conserved.

There are two types of collisions: elastic and inelastic. The difference between the two lies in whether kinetic energy is conserved. If the total kinetic energy of the system is conserved, the collision is elastic. Visually, elastic collisions are collisions in which objects bounce perfectly. If some of the kinetic energy is transformed into heat or another form of energy, the collision is inelastic. Visually, inelastic collisions are collisions in which the objects stick to each other or bounce but do not return to their original height.

If the two bodies involved in an elastic collision have the same mass, then the body that was moving will stop completely, and the body that was at rest will begin moving at the same velocity as the projectile was moving before the collision.

Fluids

FLUIDS

Concept: Liquids and gasses

A few of the questions on the exam will probably require you to consider the behavior of fluids. It sounds obvious, perhaps, but fluids can best be defined as substances that flow. A fluid will conform, slowly or quickly, to any container in which it is placed. Both liquids and gasses are considered to be fluids. Fluids are essentially those substances in which the atoms are not arranged in any permanent, rigid way. In ice, for instance, atoms are all lined up in what is known as a crystalline lattice, while in water and steam, the only intermolecular arrangements are haphazard connections between neighboring molecules.

FLOW RATES

When liquids flow in and out of containers at certain rates, the change in volume is the volumetric flow in minus the volumetric flow out. Volumetric flow is essentially the amount of volume moved past some point divided by the time it took for the volume to pass.

$$\textbf{Volumetric flow rate} = \frac{\textbf{volume moved}}{\textbf{time for the movement}}$$

If the flow into a container is greater than the flow out, the container will fill with the fluid. However, if the flow out of a container is greater than the flow into a container, the container will drain of the fluid.

57

DENSITY

Concept: How much mass is in a specific volume of a substance

Calculation: Density $= \rho = \dfrac{\text{mass}}{\text{volume}}$

Density is essentially how much stuff there is in a volume or space. The density of a fluid is generally expressed with the symbol ρ (the Greek letter *rho*). Density is a scalar property, meaning that it has no direction component.

PRESSURE

Concept: The amount of force applied per area

Calculation: Pressure $= \dfrac{\text{force}}{\text{area}}$

Pressure, like fluid density, is a scalar and does not have a direction. The equation for pressure is concerned only with the magnitude of that force, not with the direction in which it is pointing. The SI unit of pressure is the Newton per square meter, or Pascal.

As every deep-sea diver knows, the pressure of water becomes greater the deeper you go below the surface; conversely, experienced mountain climbers know that air pressure decreases as they gain a higher altitude. These pressures are typically referred to as hydrostatic pressures because they involve fluids at rest.

PASCAL'S PRINCIPLE

The exam may also require you to demonstrate some knowledge of how fluids move. Anytime you squeeze a tube of toothpaste, you are demonstrating the idea known as Pascal's principle. This principle states that a change in the pressure applied to an enclosed fluid is transmitted undiminished to every portion of the fluid as well as to the walls of the containing vessel.

BUOYANT FORCE

If an object is submerged in water, it will have a buoyant force exerted on it in the upward direction. Often, of course, this buoyant force is much too small to keep an object from sinking to the bottom. Buoyancy is summarized in Archimedes' principle; a body wholly or partially submerged in a fluid will be buoyed up by a force equal to the weight of the fluid that the body displaces.

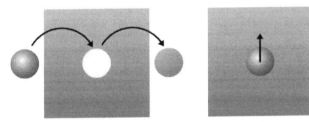

If the buoyant force is greater than the weight of an object, the object will go upward. If the weight of the object is greater than the buoyant force, the object will sink. When an object is floating on the surface, the buoyant force has the same magnitude as the weight.

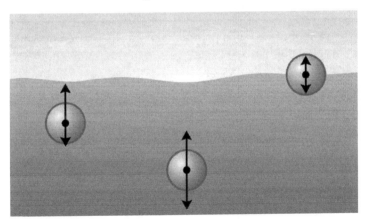

Even though the weight of a floating object is precisely balanced by a buoyant force, these forces will not necessarily act at the same point. The weight will act from the center of mass of the object, while the buoyancy will act from the center of mass of the hole in the water made by the object (known as the center of buoyancy). If the floating object is tilted, then the center of buoyancy will

59

shift and the object may be unstable. In order to remain in equilibrium, the center of buoyancy must always shift in such a way that the buoyant force and weight provide a restoring torque, one that will restore the body to its upright position. This concept is, of course, crucial to the construction of boats which must always be made to encourage restoring torque.

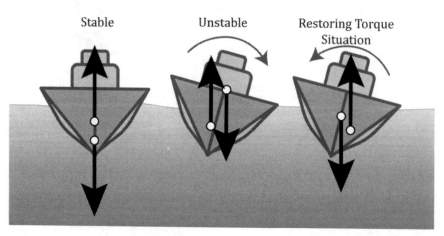

IDEAL FLUIDS

Because the motion of actual fluids is extremely complex, the exam usually assumes ideal fluids when they set up their problems. Using ideal fluids in fluid dynamics problems is like discounting friction in other problems. Therefore, when we deal with ideal fluids, we are making four assumptions. It is important to keep these in mind when considering the behavior of fluids on the exam. First, we are assuming that the flow is steady; in other words, the velocity of every part of the fluid is the same. Second, we assume that fluids are incompressible and therefore have a consistent density. Third, we assume that fluids are nonviscous, meaning that they flow easily and without resistance. Fourth, we assume that the flow of ideal fluids is irrotational: that is, particles in the fluid will not rotate around a center of mass.

BERNOULLI'S PRINCIPLE

When fluids move, they do not create or destroy energy; this modification of Newton's second law for fluid behavior is called Bernoulli's principle. It is essentially just a reformulation of the law of conservation of mechanical energy for fluid mechanics.

The most common application of Bernoulli's principle is that pressure and speed are inversely related, assuming constant altitude. Thus, if the elevation of the fluid remains constant and the speed of a fluid particle increases as it travels along a streamline, the pressure will decrease. If the fluid slows down, the pressure will increase.

Speed   Pressure

High

Low

Heat Transfer

HEAT TRANSFER

Heat is a type of energy. Heat transfers from the hot object to the cold object through the three forms of heat transfer: conduction, convection, and radiation.

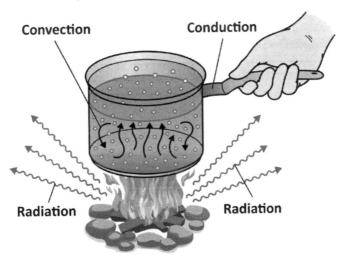

Conduction is the transfer of heat by physical contact. When you touch a hot pot, the pot transfers heat to your hand by conduction.

Convection is the transfer of heat by the movement of fluids. When you put your hand in steam, the steam transfers heat to your hand by convection.

Radiation is the transfer of heat by electromagnetic waves. When you put your hand near a campfire, the fire heats your hand by radiation.

Review Video: <u>Heat Transfer</u> Visit mometrix.com/academy and enter code: 451646

PHASE CHANGES

Materials exist in four phases or states: solid, liquid, gas, and plasma. However, as most tests will not cover plasma, we will focus on solids, liquids, and gases. The solid state is the densest in almost all cases (water is the most notable exception), followed by liquid, and then gas.

The catalyst for phase change (changing from one phase to another) is heat. When a solid is heated, it will change into a liquid. The same process of heating will change a liquid into a gas.

Optics

OPTICS

Lenses change the way light travels. Lenses are able to achieve this by the way in which light travels at different speeds in different mediums. The essentials to optics with lenses deal with concave and convex lenses. Concave lenses make objects appear smaller, while convex lenses make objects appear larger.

Convex Lens

View through a convex lens

Concave Lens

View through a concave lens

Electricity

ELECTRIC CHARGE

Much like gravity, electricity is an everyday observable phenomenon which is very complex, but may be understood as a set of behaviors. As the gravitational force exists between objects with mass, the electric force exists between objects with electrical charge. In all atoms, the protons have a positive charge, while the electrons have a negative charge. An imbalance of electrons and protons in an object results in a net charge. Unlike gravity, which only pulls, electrical forces can push objects apart as well as pull them together.

Similar electric charges repel each other. Opposite charges attract each other.

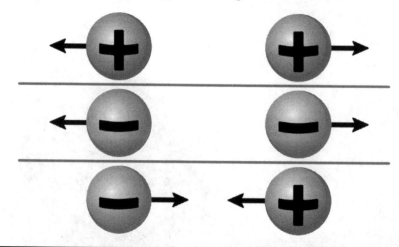

Review Video: Electric Charge
Visit mometrix.com/academy and enter code: 323587

CURRENT

Electrons (and electrical charge with it) move through conductive materials by switching quickly from one atom to another. This electrical flow can manipulate energy like mechanical systems.

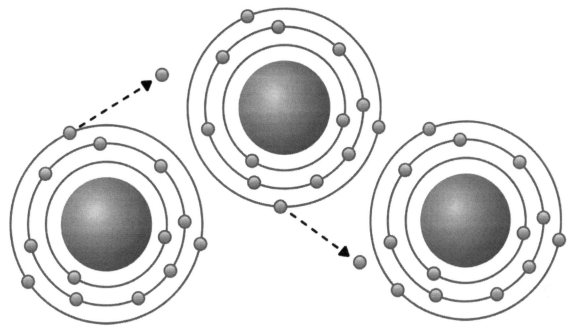

The term for the rate at which the charge flows through a conductive material is *current*. Because each electron carries a specific charge, current can be thought of as the number of electrons passing a point in a length of time. Current is measured in Amperes (A), each unit of which is approximately 6.24×10^{18} electrons per second.

Electric current carries energy much like moving balls carry energy.

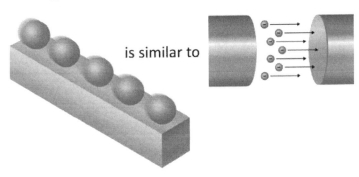

is similar to

VOLTAGE

Voltage is the potential for electric work. It can also be thought of as the *push* behind electrical work. Voltage is similar to gravitational potential energy.

is similar to

Anything used to generate a voltage, such as a battery or a generator, is called a voltage source. Voltage is conveniently measured in Volts (V).

RESISTANCE

Resistance is the amount something hinders the flow of electrical current. Electrical resistance is much like friction, resisting flow and dissipating energy.

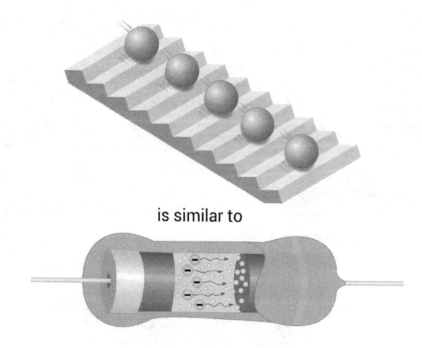

is similar to

Different objects have different resistances. A resistor is an electrical component designed to have a specific resistance, measured in Ohms (Ω).

> **Review Video: <u>Resistance of Electric Currents</u>**
> Visit mometrix.com/academy and enter code: 668423

BASIC CIRCUITS

A circuit is a closed loop through which current can flow. A simple circuit contains a voltage source and a resistor. The current flows from the positive side of the voltage source through the resistor to the negative side of the voltage source.

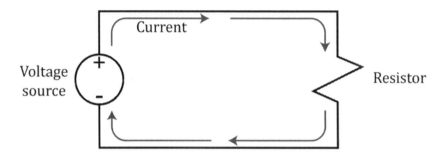

If we plot the voltage of a simple circuit, the similarities to gravitational potential energy appear.

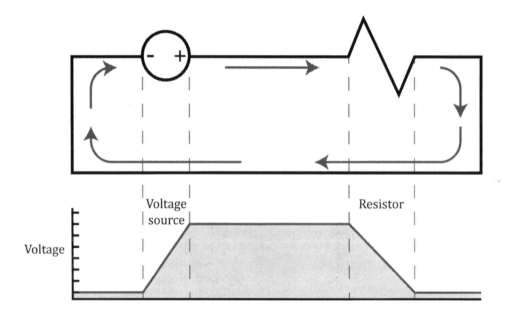

If we consider the circuit to be a track, the electrons would be balls, the voltage source would be a powered lift, and the resistor would be a sticky section of the track. The lift raises the balls, increasing their potential energy. This potential energy is expended as the balls roll down the sticky section of the track.

Voltage Source

Resistor

OHM'S LAW

A principle called Ohm's Law explains the relationship between the voltage, current, and resistance. The voltage drop over a resistance is equal to the amount of current times the resistance:

Voltage (V) = current (I) × resistance (R)

We can gain a better understanding of this equation by looking at a reference simple circuit and then changing one variable at a time to examine the results.

Voltage = Current * Resistance
1V = 1A * 1Ω

Increased Resistance | Increased Current | Increased Voltage

Voltage = Current * Resistance
1V = 0.25A * 4Ω

Voltage = Current * Resistance
1V = 4A * 0.25Ω

Voltage = Current * Resistance
4V = 2A * 2Ω

SERIES CIRCUITS

A series circuit is a circuit with two or more resistors on the same path. The same current runs through both resistors. However, the total voltage drop splits between the resistors. The resistors in series can be added together to make an equivalent basic circuit.

$$R_{equiv} = R_1 + R_2$$

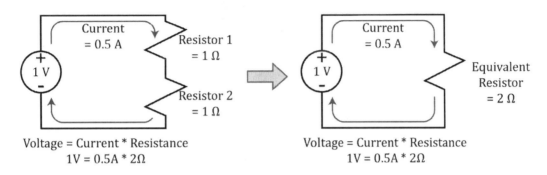

Voltage = Current * Resistance   Voltage = Current * Resistance
1V = 0.5A * 2Ω   1V = 0.5A * 2Ω

PARALLEL CIRCUITS

A parallel circuit is a circuit with two or more resistors on different, parallel paths. Unlike the series circuit, the current splits between the different paths in a parallel circuit. Resistors in parallel can be reduced to an equivalent circuit, but not by simply adding the resistances. The inverse of the equivalent resistance of parallel resistors is equal to the sum of the inverses of the resistance of each leg of the parallel circuit. In equation form that means:

$$\frac{1}{R_{equiv}} = \frac{1}{R_1} + \frac{1}{R_2}$$

Or when solved for equivalent resistance:

$$R_{equiv} = \frac{1}{\frac{1}{R_1} + \frac{1}{R_2}}$$

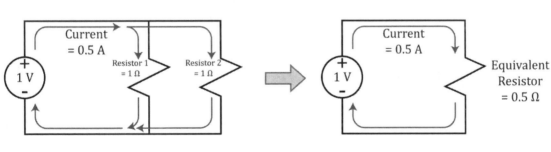

$$R_{equiv} = \frac{1}{\frac{1}{1\,\Omega} + \frac{1}{1\,\Omega}} = 0.5\,\Omega$$

ELECTRICAL POWER

Electrical power, or the energy output over time, is equal to the current resulting from a voltage source times the voltage of that source:

$$\textbf{Power(P)} = \textbf{current (I)} \times \textbf{voltage (V)}$$

Thanks to Ohm's Law, we can write this relation in two other ways:

$$P = I^2R$$

$$P = \frac{V^2}{R}$$

For instance, if a circuit is composed of a 9 Volt battery and a 3 Ohm resistor, the power output of the battery will be:

$$Power = \frac{V^2}{R} = \frac{9^2}{3} = 27\ Watts$$

AC VS. DC

Up until this point, current has been assumed to flow in one direction. One directional flow is called Direct Current (DC). However, there is another type of electric current: Alternating Current (AC). Many circuits use AC power sources, in which the current flips back and forth rapidly between directions.

Direct Current (DC)　　　　Alternating Current (AC)

CAPACITORS

Capacitors are electrical components which store voltage. Capacitors are made from two conductive surfaces separated from each other by a space and/or insulation. Capacitors resist changes to voltage. Capacitors don't stop AC circuits (although they do affect the current flow), but they do stop DC circuits, acting as open circuits.

INDUCTORS

Inductors are electrical components which effectively store current. Inductors use the relationship between electricity and magnetism to resist changes in current by running the current through coils of wire. Inductors don't stop DC circuits, but they do resist AC circuits as AC circuits utilize changing currents.

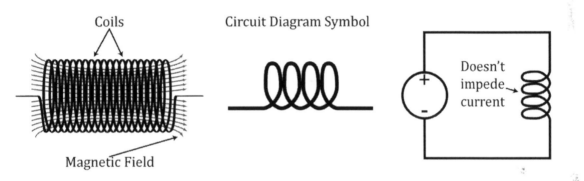

DIODES

Diodes are electrical components which limit the flow of electricity to one direction. If current flows through a diode in the intended direction, the diode will allow the flow. However, a diode will stop current if it runs the wrong way.

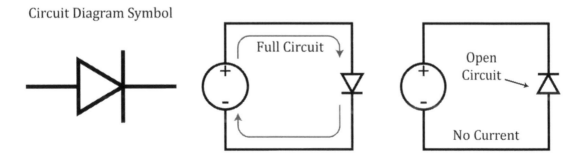

Magnetism

MAGNETISM

Magnetism is an attraction between opposite poles of magnetic materials and a repulsion between similar poles of magnetic materials. Magnetism can be natural or induced with the use of electric currents. Magnets almost always exist with two polar sides: north and south. A magnetic force exists between two poles on objects. Different poles attract each other. Like poles repel each other.

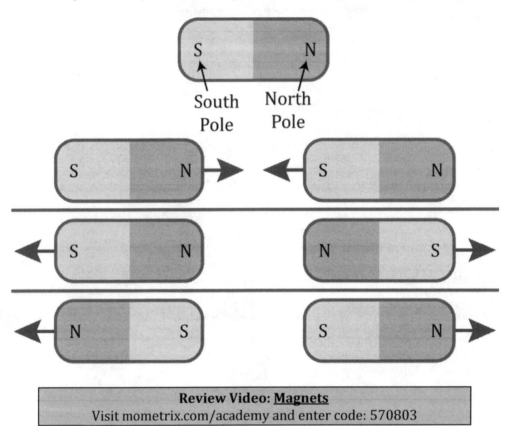

Review Video: <u>Magnets</u>
Visit mometrix.com/academy and enter code: 570803

Chapter Quiz

Ready to see how well you retained what you just read? Scan the QR code to go directly to the chapter quiz interface for this study guide. If you're using a computer, simply visit the bonus page at **<u>mometrix.com/bonus948/cast</u>** and click the Chapter Quizzes link.

The Reading Comprehension Test

Transform passive reading into active learning! After immersing yourself in this chapter, put your comprehension to the test by taking a quiz. The insights you gained will stay with you longer this way. Scan the QR code to go directly to the chapter quiz interface for this study guide. If you're using a computer, simply visit the bonus page at **mometrix.com/bonus948/cast** and click the Chapter Quizzes link.

Every CAST examination will contain some reading comprehension questions. Although critical reading skills are not normally considered to be part of the repertoire of a skilled tradesman, in actuality you will be required to read and understand a number of different texts during the course of your service. For one thing, you will often have to engage in written correspondence with your employer or with your employees. You need to be able to understand written directions and descriptions of proposed work. You will also have to stay abreast of the latest techniques and products available in your field, and for this you will need to be able to read and understand catalogs and training manuals. Finally, you may need to read local, state, and national regulations and building codes in order to avoid violating the law. The area in which you work may be heavily regulated by the government, so it is no exaggeration to say that your livelihood may depend on your ability to understand what you read.

With this in mind, let's take a look at the reading comprehension questions that will appear on the CAST exam. As mentioned above, the reading comprehension section will include 32 multiple-choice questions that must be completed within 30 minutes. These questions will be based on four passages of several paragraphs each. These passages will pertain to topics related to construction and the skilled trades. The reading comprehension exercises on the exam are designed to assess your ability to read carefully, analyze the relationships among different parts of a passage, and draw inferences from the material in the passage. The reading comprehension questions on the exam are of four basic types (main idea, detail, tone, and extending the author's reasoning), each of which calls for a slightly different approach.

The format of reading comprehension questions should not pose any problems. Each of the four passages will be followed by eight questions. These questions will be in a multiple-choice format, with four or five possible correct answers. For the most part, questions pertaining to the beginning of the passage will come before questions pertaining to the end of the passage. The reading comprehension questions on the exam are meant to be comprehensible to a general audience, and will not contain any specialized jargon. Also, all of the information required to answer the questions will be found in the passages; you will not need any outside information or experience. Now, let's take a quick look at the content of the passages that will appear on the exam.

The reading comprehension passages on CAST exams are all on subjects related to construction and the skilled trades, though they may come from a number of different genres. At least one of the passages will be an excerpt from a training manual of some kind. This passage will feature clear, technical language and a strict attention to organization. Training manuals outline the steps in a process and tend to proceed in a clear and orderly fashion. Some passages will be written in a legal style and will pertain to building regulations or codes. These passages will be dense and full of information; you are likely to be asked to recall specific details. When you are confronted with an extremely technical passage, do not feel that you have to memorize all of the details. Simply remember where the information is located in the passage so that you can refer back to it in the

73

future. A final type of passage will be a biographical account of some famous inventor or tradesman. These passages are designed to be entertaining, and will likely include colorful descriptions and interesting anecdotes. When you are presented with a passage of this type, it is likely that you will be asked to describe the author's attitude towards his or her subject.

Now that we have covered the content areas from which the reading comprehension passages will be drawn, let us consider the types of questions that you will encounter. The first and most basic kind of reading comprehension question is the one that asks you to define the main idea of the passage. This question may arrive in any of a few different forms. The question may ask you for the "the best summary," the "salient point," or the "overarching theme" of the passage. Do not be flummoxed by the precise language; this is a main idea question. And, as you no doubt have learned by now, the main idea of a passage is most likely to appear in either the first or the last sentence. So, as you are reading a passage for the first time, pay special attention to the beginning and end. Whether the main idea is offered first or last will depend on the type of passage: expository passages tend to give a main idea first and then spend the rest of the sentences defending it, while critical or argumentative essays will often begin with a set of loose facts and end with a summarizing conclusion. In any case, be prepared to refer back to the text in search of the main idea.

On occasion, the authors of the exam will try to fool you by asking you to provide the main idea of a specific *part* of the passage rather than of the passage as a whole. Similarly, they may try to confuse you with answer choices that are true without being the main idea of the passage. For this reason, it is imperative that you read the question carefully and do not just assume that the first or last sentence of the paragraph is the main idea. The main idea is not just any true statement contained within the passage; it is the idea that most effectively summarizes the entire passage.

It is certain that at least a couple of the reading comprehension questions will ask you to determine the main idea. In addition, it is quite likely that a few of the questions will ask you to recall specific details from the passage. This would appear to be the easiest kind of question to answer, but many students go astray by relying on memory instead of scrolling back up to find the pertinent details in the passage. Remember that you are free to refer to the text as much as you like. Also, remember that specific questions are likely to have specific answers, just as general questions are likely to have general answers. In other words, if the question asks you to name a concept, the answer probably will not be a piece of specific data.

A more subtle form of question is the one that requires you to diagnose the author's attitude. As with the main idea question, this kind of question can take a number of different forms. It may ask you to describe the tone, opinion, feeling, or mood of the author or passage. All of these questions are essentially asking you to assess how the author feels about his or her topic. In order to answer such a question, you will have to pay attention to the specific language used by the author, and the point of view that the language conveys. For instance, if the author is describing a small person, he or she would create a sharply different tone by using the word *puny* than by using the word *petite*. *Puny* suggests a shriveled, scrawny individual, while *petite* conjures daintiness and delicacy. It may take a little bit of practice before you habitually notice these shades of meaning, but you should try to be conscious of the ways in which language can be used to subtly indicate attitude. For the most part, the test administrators avoid passages that are violently opinionated or controversial. Any answer choices that suggest the author holds an opinion which could be considered radical or offensive are most likely incorrect.

The final category of question which you may encounter on the exam is one that asks you to extend the author's reasoning. Put another way, these questions require you to consider the information provided in the passage and then use this information to consider a problem not mentioned in the passage. The reasoning required to answer these kinds of questions will not be extremely complicated. The most common problem students have with questions asking them to extend the reasoning of the passage is that they attempt to find the answer explicitly in the passage. Remember that even though all of the information needed to answer every question can be found in the text, some questions will require you to do some independent thinking.

The best way to prepare for the reading comprehension section of the written examination is to practice reading a variety of different texts. By visiting the local library, you should be able to obtain journal articles and training manuals. As you read these texts, practice finding the main idea and identifying key details. You may want to practice scanning a short passage to determine the basic structure, before you go back and read in more detail. You will be allowed to make notes and underline on the written examination, so feel free to do this during your practice if it helps you to understand the text.

Time-Saving Tips

SKIMMING

Your first task when you begin reading is to answer the question "What is the topic of the selection?" This can best be answered by quickly skimming the passage for the general idea, stopping to read only the first sentence of each paragraph. A paragraph's first sentence is usually the main topic sentence, and it gives you a summary of the content of the paragraph.

Once you've skimmed the passage, stopping to read only the first sentences, you will have a general idea about what it is about, as well as what is the expected topic in each paragraph.

Each question will contain clues as to where to find the answer in the passage. Do not just randomly search through the passage for the correct answer to each question. Search scientifically. Find key words or ideas in the question that are going to either contain or be near the correct answer. These are typically nouns, verbs, numbers, or phrases in the question that will probably be duplicated in the passage. Once you have identified the key words or ideas, skim the passage quickly to find where the key words or ideas appear. The correct answer choice will be nearby.

Example: What caused Martin to suddenly return to Paris?

The key word is *Paris*. Skim the passage quickly to find where this word appears. The answer will be close by that word.

However, sometimes key words in the question are not repeated in the passage. In those cases, search for the general idea of the question.

Example: Which of the following was the psychological impact of the author's childhood upon the remainder of his life?

Key words are *childhood* or *psychology*. While searching for those words, be alert for other words or phrases that have similar meaning, such as *emotional effect* or *mentally* which could be used in the passage, rather than the exact word *psychology*.

75

Numbers or years can be particularly good key words to skim for, as they stand out from the rest of the text.

> Example: Which of the following best describes the influence of Newton's work in the 20th century?

The adjective *20th* contains numbers and will easily stand out from the rest of the text. Use *20th* as the key word to skim for in the passage.

Other good key words may be in quotation marks. These identify a word or phrase that is copied directly from the passage. In those cases, the words in quotation marks are exactly duplicated in the passage.

> Example: In her college years, what was meant by Margaret's "drive for excellence"?

"Drive for excellence" is a direct quote from the passage and should be easy to find.

Once you've quickly found the correct section of the passage to find the answer, focus upon the answer choices. Sometimes a choice will repeat word for word a portion of the passage near the answer. However, beware of such duplication – it may be a trap! More than likely, the correct choice will paraphrase or summarize the related portion of the passage, rather than being exactly the same wording.

For the answers that you think are correct, read them carefully and make sure that they answer the question. An answer can be factually correct, but it MUST answer the question asked. Additionally, two answers can both be seemingly correct, so be sure to read all of the answer choices, and make sure that you get the one that BEST answers the question.

Some questions will not have a key word.

> Example: Which of the following would the author of this passage likely agree with?

In these cases, look for key words in the answer choices. Then, skim the passage to find where the answer choice occurs. By skimming to find where to look, you can minimize the time required.

Sometimes, it may be difficult to identify a good key word in the question to skim for in the passage. In those cases, look for a key word in one of the answer choices to skim for. Often, the answer choices can all be found in the same paragraph, which can quickly narrow your search.

PARAGRAPH FOCUS

Focus upon the first sentence of each paragraph, which is the most important. The main topic of the paragraph is usually there.

Once you've read the first sentence in the paragraph, you should have a general idea about what each paragraph will be about. As you read the questions, try to determine which paragraph will have the answer. Paragraphs have a concise topic. The answer should either obviously be there or obviously not. It will save time if you can jump straight to the paragraph, so try to remember what you learned from the first sentences.

> Example: The first paragraph is about radiation; the second is about cancer. If a question asks about cancer, where will the answer be? The second paragraph.

The main idea of a passage is typically spread across all or most of its paragraphs. Whereas the main idea of a paragraph may be completely different than the main idea of the very next paragraph, a main idea for a passage affects all of the paragraphs in one form or another.

>Example: What is the main idea of the passage?

For each answer choice, try to see how many paragraphs are related. It can help to count how many sentences are affected by each choice, but it is best to see how many paragraphs are affected by the choice. Typically, the answer choices will include incorrect choices that are main ideas of individual paragraphs, but not the entire passage. That is why it is crucial to choose ideas that are supported by the most paragraphs possible.

ELIMINATE CHOICES

Some choices can quickly be eliminated. "Albert Einstein lived there." Is Albert Einstein even mentioned in the passage? If not, quickly eliminate it.

When trying to answer a question such as "the passage indicates all of the following EXCEPT," quickly skim the paragraph searching for references to each choice. If the reference exists, scratch it off as a choice. Similar choices may be crossed off simultaneously if they are close enough.

In choices that ask you to choose "which answer choice does NOT describe?" or "all of the following answer choices are identifiable characteristics, EXCEPT which?", look for answers that are similarly worded. Since only one answer can be correct, if there are two answers that appear to mean the same thing, they must BOTH be incorrect and can be eliminated.

>Example:
>A.) changing values and attitudes
>B.) a large population of mobile or uprooted people

These answer choices are similar; they both describe a fluid culture. Because of their similarity, they can be linked together. Since the answer can have only one choice, they can also be eliminated together.

CONTEXTUAL CLUES

Look for contextual clues. An answer can be right but not correct. The contextual clues will help you find the answer that is most right and is correct. Understand the context in which a phrase is stated.

When asked for the implied meaning of a statement made in the passage, immediately go find the statement and read the context it was made in. Also, look for an answer choice that has a similar phrase to the statement in question.

>Example: In the passage, what is implied by the phrase "Scientists have become more or less part of the furniture"?

Find an answer choice that is similar or describes the phrase "part of the furniture," as that is the key phrase in the question. "Part of the furniture" is a saying that means something is fixed, immovable, or set in its ways. Those are all similar ways of saying "part of the furniture." As such, the correct answer choice will probably include a similar rewording of the expression.

>Example: Why was John described as "morally desperate"?

The answer will probably have some sort of definition of morals in it. "Morals" refers to a code of right and wrong behavior, so the correct answer choice will likely have words that mean something like that.

FACT/OPINION

When asked about which statement is a fact or opinion, remember that answer choices that are facts will typically have no ambiguous words. For example, how long is a long time? What defines an ordinary person? These ambiguous words of *long* and *ordinary* should not be in a factual statement. However, if all of the choices have ambiguous words, go to the context of the passage. Often, a factual statement may be set out as a research finding.

> Example: "The scientist found that the eye reacts quickly to change in light."

Opinions may be set out in the context of words like *thought, believed, understood,* or *wished.*

> Example: "He thought the Yankees should win the World Series."

OPPOSITES

Answer choices that are direct opposites are usually correct. The paragraph will often contain established relationships (when this goes up, that goes down). The question may ask you to draw conclusions for this and will give two similar answer choices that are opposites.

> Example:
> A.) a decrease in housing starts
> B.) an increase in housing starts

MAKE PREDICTIONS

As you read and understand the passage and then the question, try to guess what the answer will be. Remember that all but one of the answer choices are wrong, and once you read them, your mind will immediately become cluttered with answer choices designed to throw you off. Your mind is typically the most focused immediately after you have read the passage and question and digested its contents. If you can, try to predict what the correct answer will be. You may be surprised at what you can predict.

Quickly scan the choices and see if your prediction is in the listed answer choices. If it is, then you can be quite confident that you have the right answer. It still won't hurt to check the other answer choices, but most of the time, you've got it!

ANSWER THE QUESTION

It may seem obvious to only pick answer choices that answer the question, but the test can create some excellent answer choices that are wrong. Don't pick an answer just because it sounds right, or you believe it to be true. It MUST answer the question. Once you've made your selection, always go back and check it against the question and make sure that you didn't misread the question, and the answer choice does answer the question posed.

BENCHMARK

After you read the first answer choice, decide if you think it sounds correct or not. If it doesn't, move on to the next answer choice. If it does, make a mental note about that choice. This doesn't mean that you've definitely selected it as your answer choice, it just means that it's the best you've seen thus far. Go ahead and read the next choice. If the next choice is worse than the one you've already selected, keep going to the next answer choice. If the next choice is better than the choice you've already selected, then make a mental note about that answer choice.

As you read through the list, you are mentally noting the choice you think is right. That is your new standard. Every other answer choice must be benchmarked against that standard. That choice is correct until proven otherwise by another answer choice beating it out. Once you've decided that no other answer choice seems as good, do one final check to ensure that it answers the question posed.

New Information

Correct answers will usually contain the information listed in the paragraph and question. Rarely will completely new information be inserted into a correct answer choice. Occasionally the new information may be related in a manner that the test is asking for you to interpret, but seldom.

> Example:
> The argument above is dependent upon which of the following assumptions?
> A.) Charles's Law was used

If Charles's Law is not mentioned at all in the referenced paragraph and argument, then it is unlikely that this choice is correct. All of the information needed to answer the question is provided for you, so you should not have to make guesses that are unsupported or choose answer choices that have unknown information that cannot be reasoned.

Valid Information

Don't discount any of the information provided in the passage, particularly shorter ones. Every piece of information may be necessary to determine the correct answer. None of the information in the paragraph is there to throw you off (while the answer choices will certainly have information to throw you off). If two seemingly unrelated topics are discussed, don't ignore either. You can be confident there is a relationship, or it wouldn't be included in the paragraph, and you are probably going to have to determine what is that relationship for the answer.

Time Management

In technical passages, do not get lost on the technical terms. Skip them and move on. You want a general understanding of what is going on, not a mastery of the passage.

When you encounter material in the selection that seems difficult to understand, it often may not be necessary and can be skipped. Only spend time trying to understand it if it is going to be relevant for a question. Understand difficult phrases only as a last resort.

Answer general questions before detail questions. A reader with a good understanding of the whole passage can often answer general questions without rereading a word. Get the easier questions out of the way before tackling the more time consuming ones.

Identify each question by type. Usually the wording of a question will tell you whether you can find the answer by referring directly to the passage or by using your reasoning powers. You alone know which question types you customarily handle with ease and which give you trouble and will require more time. Save the difficult questions for last.

Final Warnings

WORD USAGE QUESTIONS

When asked how a word is used in the passage, don't use your existing knowledge of the word. The question is being asked precisely because there is some strange or unusual usage of the word in the passage. Go to the passage and use contextual clues to determine the answer. Don't simply use the popular definition you already know.

SWITCHBACK WORDS

Stay alert for "switchbacks". These are the words and phrases frequently used to alert you to shifts in thought. The most common switchback word is "but". Others include although, however, nevertheless, on the other hand, even though, while, in spite of, despite, regardless of.

AVOID "FACT TRAPS"

Once you know which paragraph the answer will be in, focus on that paragraph. However, don't get distracted by a choice that is factually true about the paragraph. Your search is for the answer that answers the question, which may be about a tiny aspect in the paragraph. Stay focused and don't fall for an answer that describes the larger picture of the paragraph. Always go back to the question and make sure you're choosing an answer that actually answers the question and is not just a true statement.

Chapter Quiz

Ready to see how well you retained what you just read? Scan the QR code to go directly to the chapter quiz interface for this study guide. If you're using a computer, simply visit the bonus page at **mometrix.com/bonus948/cast** and click the Chapter Quizzes link.

The Mathematical Usage Test

Transform passive reading into active learning! After immersing yourself in this chapter, put your comprehension to the test by taking a quiz. The insights you gained will stay with you longer this way. Scan the QR code to go directly to the chapter quiz interface for this study guide. If you're using a computer, simply visit the bonus page at **mometrix.com/bonus948/cast** and click the Chapter Quizzes link.

If you were hoping to avoid dealing with math by becoming a skilled tradesman, you may be disappointed when you sit for the CAST exam. The good news though is that there is only one type of question in the mathematical usage section: unit conversions. With a little bit of a refresher and a lot of practice, you should have no problem with this section of the exam.

This section has 18 questions and a 7-minute time limit.

WHAT DO THE MATHEMATICAL USAGE QUESTIONS LOOK LIKE?

Each mathematical usage question will give you a measurement in one set of units and ask you for the equivalent measurement in a different set of units. For instance, you may be given a distance in feet and asked what the equivalent is in miles. Don't worry about memorizing conversion ratios; you will be given a table on the test with all of the unit conversions you will need to answer the questions. In some ways, finding the applicable conversion factor on the list can be the hardest part since it is a long list and not necessarily formatted in a way that is easy to read. Many of the units included on the test will be familiar to you, but there will also be some obscure units you may have never heard of, like chains, gills, and rods.

The questions are in a multiple-choice format, with five possible answers to choose from, including N (none of the above). Calculators are not allowed, but that means that most of the calculations are simpler than they appear. For instance, you might be asked to convert 15,840 feet into miles. This seems complicated at first glance because it's a 5-digit number, but when you realize that most of the questions have whole-number answer choices, it becomes a lot easier. In this case, the answer is 3 miles because $15,840 \div 5,280 = 3$.

Most of these questions will require only one conversion step, meaning that there is a unit conversion provided on the list that contains both the given unit and the required unit. However, this will not be the case for the last few questions in this section. For these, you will have to string together two conversion ratios: one that converts from the given unit to a unit not mentioned in the question and one that converts from that new unit to the required unit. For instance, you may be asked to convert centimeters to yards. There is no direct conversion between centimeters and yards given, but there is a conversion between centimeters and inches and another conversion given between inches and yards.

WHAT STRATEGIES CAN I USE?

With math questions, there aren't usually a lot of special strategies. You solve the problem and get the correct answer. Here though, there is a legitimate shortcut for some of the questions: **Always look at the answer choices first**. In many cases, either the number of the given units or the answer in required units will be a small whole number. This is especially true if the other number has several digits. The answer choices are often far enough apart that you can figure out the answer just by estimating from the conversion rate.

How Do I Solve These Questions?

Let's start with some basic math knowledge:

A **fraction** is a number that is expressed as one integer written above another integer, with a dividing line between them $\left(\frac{x}{y}\right)$. It represents the **quotient** of the two numbers, "x divided by y." It can also be thought of as x out of y equal parts.

The top number of a fraction is called the **numerator**, and it represents the number of parts under consideration. The 1 in $\frac{1}{4}$ means that 1 part out of the whole is being considered in the calculation. The bottom number of a fraction is called the **denominator**, and it represents the total number of equal parts. The 4 in $\frac{1}{4}$ means that the whole consists of 4 equal parts. A fraction cannot have a denominator of zero; this is referred to as "undefined."

How Does This Relate to Unit Conversions?

When the numerator and the denominator are the same number, the value of the fraction is 1. You can multiply any number by 1 and the result is the original number. Similarly, you can multiply any number by a fraction that has the same value in the numerator and the denominator, and the result is the same value as the original number.

This is the principle that makes unit conversions work. When we are applying a unit conversion, we are multiplying a measurement by a fraction that has the same value in the numerator and the denominator. These values are simply stated in different units:

$$\frac{1 \text{ foot}}{12 \text{ inches}} = \frac{12 \text{ inches}}{1 \text{ foot}} = 1$$

$$\frac{1 \text{ mile}}{5{,}280 \text{ feet}} = \frac{5{,}280 \text{ feet}}{1 \text{ mile}} = 1$$

If we need to know what 4 miles is in feet, we can set up an equation to solve that:

$$4 \text{ miles } \times \frac{5{,}280 \text{ feet}}{1 \text{ mile}} = (4 \times 5{,}280) \text{ feet} = 21{,}120 \text{ feet}$$

If we need to know what 108 inches is in feet, we can set up an equation to solve that:

$$108 \text{ inches} \times \frac{1 \text{ foot}}{12 \text{ inches}} = (108 \div 12) \text{ feet} = 9 \text{ feet}$$

When setting up unit conversion equations, keep in mind that the unit you are *already in* goes on the *bottom* of the fraction and the unit you are *moving to* goes on the *top* of the fraction.

What Other Math Do I Need to Know?

Once you set up your unit conversion, you have to solve it, which means either multiplying or dividing. As we've already covered, you don't get a calculator, but they've tried to make the calculations simple enough that you shouldn't need one. If you want to be prepared, just in case you do end up needing to do some brute force calculations on the test, review the following sections.

MULTIPLICATION OF LARGE NUMBERS

The process of multiplying two large numbers involves many steps. For this example, we will look at multiplying two three-digit numbers. Each digit from one number is individually multiplied by each digit from the other number, and the products are added together.

<u>EXAMPLE</u>

Demonstrate how to multiply 525 and 189.

First, set up the multiplication problem:

$$
\begin{array}{r}
525 \\
\times \quad 189 \\
\hline
\end{array}
$$

We will approach the task of multiplying each pair of digits by starting with the ones digit of the bottom number and multiplying it by each digit of the top number, starting on the right (9×5), As with the process of addition, when the result is a two-digit number, we place the last digit in the column below the numbers we have multiplied and place the other above the next column to the left:

$$
\begin{array}{r}
\mathbf{4} \quad \\
5 \quad 2 \quad 5 \\
\times \quad 1 \quad 8 \quad 9 \\
\hline
\mathbf{5}
\end{array}
$$

After we multiply the next pair of numbers, we will add to that the 4 that we placed above the tens column ($9 \times 2 + 4$):

$$
\begin{array}{r}
\mathbf{2} \quad \mathbf{4} \quad \\
5 \quad \mathbf{2} \quad 5 \\
\times \quad 1 \quad 8 \quad \mathbf{9} \\
\hline
\mathbf{2} \quad 5
\end{array}
$$

Repeat this process for the next pair ($9 \times 5 + 2$), but instead of placing it above, since there isn't another column of numbers to the left, place it below the line:

$$
\begin{array}{r}
2 \quad 4 \quad \\
\mathbf{5} \quad 2 \quad 5 \\
\times \quad 1 \quad 8 \quad \mathbf{9} \\
\hline
\mathbf{4} \quad \mathbf{7} \quad 2 \quad 5
\end{array}
$$

Before we move on to multiplying the top number by the tens digit of the bottom number, we need to clear out the numbers we wrote above the top number. Then we can proceed to multiply the next sets of digits (8×5):

$$
\begin{array}{r}
\mathbf{4} \quad \\
5 \quad 2 \quad \mathbf{5} \\
\times \quad 1 \quad \mathbf{8} \quad 9 \\
\hline
4 \quad 7 \quad 2 \quad 5 \\
\mathbf{0}
\end{array}
$$

Note that we do not place any numbers in the rightmost column (the ones column) of the bottom row since we are multiplying by a digit in the tens column this time. Proceed as before to the next pair of digits ($8 \times 2 + 4$):

```
    2 4
    5 2 5
×   1 8 9
  4 7 2 5
    0 0
```

Once again, when we run out of columns to place the extra digit over, we make room for it below the line ($8 \times 5 + 2$):

```
      2 4
      5 2 5
×     1 8 9
    4 7 2 5
  4 2 0 0
```

Next, we clear the numbers above and move on to multiplying the top number by the hundreds digit of the bottom number, this time starting in the hundreds column when writing our answer:

```
      5 2 5
×     1 8 9
    4 7 2 5
  4 2 0 0
  5 2 5
```

Now that we've completed the multiplication steps, we must add all of the numbers below the line. Add a 0 to every column that has a number filled in to the left of it, and set up an addition problem:

```
      4 7 2 5
    4 2 0 0 0
  + 5 2 5 0 0
```

Perform the addition steps:

```
    1
      4 7 2 5
    4 2 0 0 0
  + 5 2 5 0 0
    9 9 2 2 5
```

Thus, we see that $525 \times 189 = 99{,}225$.

LONG DIVISION

Unlike all of the other basic operations involving multi-digit numbers, long division begins on the left-hand side and moves right. The process can be best explained by working through an example.

EXAMPLE

Demonstrate how to divide 8,192 by 32.

First, set up the division problem. The first number goes under the line, and second number goes on the same row but to the left of the vertical line:

$$32 \,\big|\, 8 \quad 1 \quad 9 \quad 2$$

Since the number we're trying to divide by has two digits, check to see how many times it can fit into the first two digits of the other number (if the answer is *zero*, try fitting it into the first three digits). Since 32 can fit into 81 completely 2 times, write a 2 above the 1 in the original number. Then multiply 32 by 2, write that number below the 81, and subtract it from 81:

$$
\begin{array}{r}
2 \\
32 \,\big|\, 8 \quad 1 \quad 9 \quad 2 \\
6 \quad 4 \\
\hline
1 \quad 7
\end{array}
$$

Next, bring down the next digit from the original number (9) and put it next to the result of our subtraction (17). This gives us the next number that we will try to fit 32 into:

$$
\begin{array}{r}
2 \\
32 \,\big|\, 8 \quad 1 \quad 9 \quad 2 \\
6 \quad 4 \\
\hline
1 \quad 7 \quad 9
\end{array}
$$

Since 32 can fit into 179 completely 5 times, write a 5 above the 9 in the original number. Then multiply 32 by 5, write that number below the 179, and subtract it from 179:

$$
\begin{array}{r}
2 \quad 5 \\
32 \,\big|\, 8 \quad 1 \quad 9 \quad 2 \\
6 \quad 4 \\
\hline
1 \quad 7 \quad 9 \\
1 \quad 6 \quad 0 \\
\hline
1 \quad 9
\end{array}
$$

Next, bring down the next digit from the original number (2) and put it next to the result of our subtraction (19). This gives us the next number that we will try to fit 32 into:

$$
\begin{array}{r}
2 \quad 5 \\
32 \,\big|\, 8 \quad 1 \quad 9 \quad 2 \\
6 \quad 4 \\
\hline
1 \quad 7 \quad 9 \\
1 \quad 6 \quad 0 \\
\hline
1 \quad 9 \quad 2
\end{array}
$$

Since 32 can fit into 192 completely 6 times, write a 6 above the 2 in the original number. Then multiply 32 by 6, write that number below the 192, and subtract it from 192:

```
            2   5   6
    32 |  8   1   9   2
         6   4
         _____
         1   7   9
         1   6   0
         _____
             1   9   2
             1   9   2
             _____
                     0
```

MULTIPLYING DECIMALS

A simple multiplication problem has two components: a **multiplicand** and a **multiplier**. When multiplying decimals, work as though the numbers were whole rather than decimals. Once the final product is calculated, count the number of places to the right of the decimal in both the multiplicand and the multiplier. Then, count that number of places from the right of the product and place the decimal in that position.

For example, 12.3×2.56 has a total of three places to the right of the respective decimals. Multiply 123×256 to get 31488. Now, beginning on the right, count three places to the left and insert the decimal. The final product will be 31.488.

> **Review Video: Multiplying Decimals**
> Visit mometrix.com/academy and enter code: 731574

DIVIDING DECIMALS

Every division problem has a **divisor** and a **dividend**. The dividend is the number that is being divided. In the problem $14 \div 7$, 14 is the dividend and 7 is the divisor. In a division problem with decimals, the divisor must be converted into a whole number. Begin by moving the decimal in the divisor to the right until a whole number is created. Next, move the decimal in the dividend the same number of spaces to the right. For example, $4.9 \div 24.5$ would become $49 \div 245$. The decimal was moved one space to the right to create a whole number in the divisor, and then the same was done for the dividend. Once the whole numbers are created, the problem is carried out normally: $245 \div 49 = 5$.

> **Review Video: Dividing Decimals**
> Visit mometrix.com/academy and enter code: 560690
>
> **Review Video: Dividing Decimals by Whole Numbers**
> Visit mometrix.com/academy and enter code: 535669

Chapter Quiz

Ready to see how well you retained what you just read? Scan the QR code to go directly to the chapter quiz interface for this study guide. If you're using a computer, simply visit the bonus page at **mometrix.com/bonus948/cast** and click the Chapter Quizzes link.

Graphic Arithmetic

The graphic arithmetic section of the CAST exam requires you to apply your knowledge of basic arithmetic to common scenarios in construction and the skilled trades. Specifically, the graphic arithmetic section presents you with a drawing and asks you a series of questions based on the information within it. The graphic arithmetic section consists of 16 questions and must be completed within 30 minutes. The questions will be based on two drawings. Each question will be followed by five possible answer choices; the fifth answer choice will be "N," meaning none of the above.

The good news here is that all of the mathematical knowledge required for the graphic arithmetic has been discussed in the mathematical usage section. For the most part, the graphic arithmetic section of the exam focuses on a few operations: adding, subtracting, finding area, and ratios. Since we have already covered these fundamentals, we can turn our attention to the specific kinds of problems you will encounter in the graphic arithmetic section.

The most common type of drawing featured on the graphical arithmetic section of the exam is the floor plan. Indeed, all of the drawings used in this section of the exam are either floor plans or equivalent diagrams. A basic example of a floor plan is given below.

You are no doubt familiar with this kind of diagram. This particular floor plan is for a food distribution warehouse (hence the large number of coolers). The numbers indicate the distances in feet along each wall. Although this floor plan is drawn roughly to scale, you should not expect the diagrams on your exam to be to scale. Therefore, you should only use information that is explicitly given in the picture; just because one distance appears to be greater than another does not make it so.

When you are presented with a floor plan like this, you will probably be asked a few questions requiring you to find a distance. For example, you might be asked to find the width of the recessed four truck docks. The number on the bottom of the docks is the measure of the width of the docks and the adjacent cooler, and therefore cannot be the answer. In order to find the width of the docks, you will have to perform one of two calculations. Either you will have to add the two widths on the top of the docks (24 feet and 32 feet, respectively), or you will have to take the combined length of the docks and cooler (72 feet) and subtract the width of the cooler (16 feet). Either way, you will end up with a distance of 56 feet.

Some questions will ask you to compare two distances. For example, you might be asked to calculate how much longer the cooler in the top left corner is than the cooler in the bottom right corner. Since the cooler in the top left is 50 feet long and the cooler in the bottom right is 48 feet long, subtraction indicates that the cooler in the top left is two feet longer than the cooler on the bottom right.

You will also be asked to find the area of a particular part of the floor plan. For instance, imagine that you are asked to find the area of the warm room. Remember that the formula for area is *Area = length x width*. The length of the warm room is 32 feet, and the width is 30 feet. The area, then, is 960 square feet. Some questions may ask you to combine the areas of a few different rooms; simply calculate the respective areas individually and then perform whatever operations are necessary.

In rare cases, you may be asked to find the area of an irregular-shaped room. For example, imagine you are asked to find the area of the recessed four truck docks. The best way to solve this type of problem is to break the room down into constituent quadrilaterals. The recessed four truck docks in the floor plan above can be broken down into two rectangles by extending an imaginary line out from the 24-foot wall until it intersects with the 31-foot wall. The top rectangle has a length of 21 feet and a width of 32 feet, and therefore has an area of 672 square feet. The bottom rectangle has a length of 10 feet (found by subtracting the 21-foot section from the 31-foot wall) and a width of 56 feet (found by adding the 24-foot and 32-foot walls), and therefore has an area of 560 square feet. Therefore, the total area of the recessed four truck docks is $672 + 560 = 1,232$ square feet. This kind of problem is rare on the CAST exam, but it can be solved easily if you take your time and break it down into simple steps.

Finally, you will be asked a few questions that require you to demonstrate knowledge of ratios. For instance, the test might ask you the following question: *how many times longer is the cooler in the bottom right corner than the warm room adjacent to it?* The length of the cooler is 48 feet, and the length of the warm room is 32 feet. Before we perform any simplification, then, we can state that the ratio is 48:32. But, in order to solve this problem, we will need to simplify the 32 into a 1, so that we will know how many units of cooler there are for every unit of warm room. This is accomplished by dividing each side of the ratio by 32. 32 divided by 32 is one, of course. In order to solve 48 divided by 32, you will need to convert 48 into 48.0. Once this is done, you should derive a result of 1.5. In other words, the cooler is 1.5 times as long as the warm room.

There is another way in which ratios can appear on the graphic arithmetic section of the CAST. For instance, imagine the question was phrased this way: *what is the ratio between the length of the bottom-right cooler and the length of the warm room adjacent?* If the problem is phrased this way, you will need to perform a slightly different operation on the ratio 48:32. Instead of dividing both sides by 32, you can find the greatest common factor of each number and divide by that. Remember that the greatest common factor is the largest number that both sides of the ratio can be divided by evenly. In this case, the greatest common factor is 16. If we divide both sides by 16, we derive the simplest form of the ratio, 3:2.

Although the graphic arithmetic section of the exam is generally considered to be the easiest component, some of these problems can be tricky. In particular, many candidates have a hard time working with ratios at first. The best way to improve your skill on the graphic arithmetic section of the exam is to find some basic floor plans on the internet and practice finding lengths, areas, and ratios. Even better, you can print out some simple floor plans and cover up various lengths and widths, and then see if you can figure out the hidden values based on the numbers that are still visible. The calculations required for this section of the exam should not be a problem; as a matter of fact, they are considerably less difficult than those you will be performing in the mathematical usage section. The most challenging thing about the graphic arithmetic section of the exam is just becoming comfortable with the style and structure of the diagrams used in construction and the skilled trades.

Chapter Quiz

Ready to see how well you retained what you just read? Scan the QR code to go directly to the chapter quiz interface for this study guide. If you're using a computer, simply visit the bonus page at **mometrix.com/bonus948/cast** and click the Chapter Quizzes link.

Appendix: Area, Volume, Surface Area Formulas

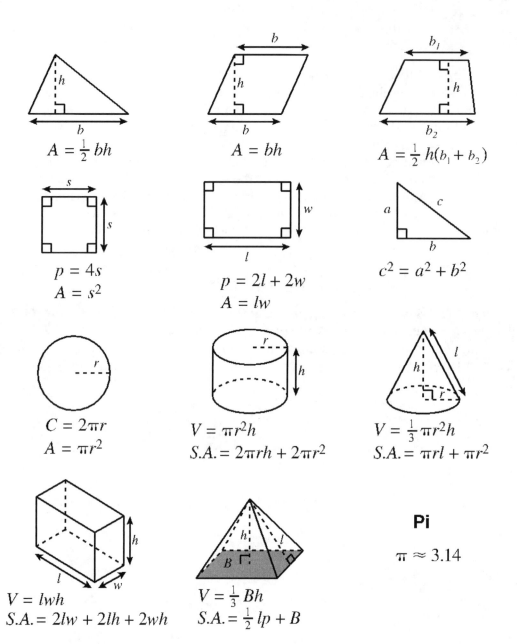

$$A = \frac{1}{2}bh$$

$$A = bh$$

$$A = \frac{1}{2}h(b_1 + b_2)$$

$$p = 4s$$
$$A = s^2$$

$$p = 2l + 2w$$
$$A = lw$$

$$c^2 = a^2 + b^2$$

$$C = 2\pi r$$
$$A = \pi r^2$$

$$V = \pi r^2 h$$
$$S.A. = 2\pi rh + 2\pi r^2$$

$$V = \frac{1}{3}\pi r^2 h$$
$$S.A. = \pi rl + \pi r^2$$

$$V = lwh$$
$$S.A. = 2lw + 2lh + 2wh$$

$$V = \frac{1}{3}Bh$$
$$S.A. = \frac{1}{2}lp + B$$

Pi

$$\pi \approx 3.14$$

90

CAST Practice Test

Want to take this practice test in an online interactive format?
Check out the bonus page, which includes interactive practice questions and
much more: **mometrix.com/bonus948/cast**

Mechanical Concepts

This is a test of your ability to understand mechanical concepts. Each question has a picture, a question and three possible answers. Read each question carefully, study the picture, and decide which answer is correct.

1. Objects 1 and 2 are submerged in separate tanks, both filled with water. In which tank (A or B) will the water level be the highest? (If equal, mark C)

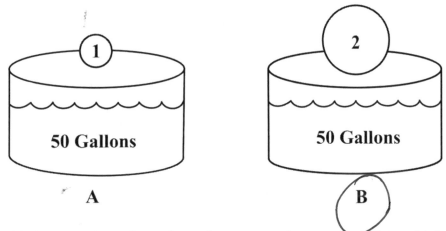

2. If ball 1 and ball 2 are of equal weight and moving at the same speed, in which direction (A, B or C) will ball 1 tend to go when it collides with ball 2 at point X?

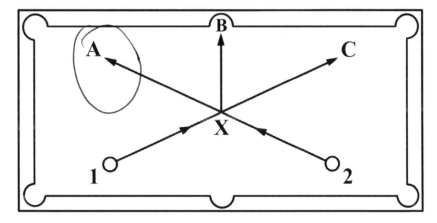

3. In which direction (A or B) will gear 5 spin if gear 1 is spinning counter-clockwise? (If both, mark C)

A) counter

4. Which of the two identical objects (A or B) will launch a higher distance when the springs are released? (If equal, mark C)

5. A watering can is filled with water. Which of the pictures (A or B) shows a more accurate representation of how the water will rest?

Mometrix

6. Among this arrangement of three pulleys, which pulley (A, B or C) turns fastest?

smallest circumference

7. Which of the two scenarios (A or B) requires more effort to pull the weight up off the ground? (If equal, mark C)

A   B

8. Which switch (A, B or C) should be closed in order to start the pump motor?

9. If both ramps are 5 feet tall, which situation (A or B) requires more force to peddle the bicycle up the ramp? (If equal, mark C)

20 Feet   A   80 Feet   B

10. When the spring is released, the ball travels away from the spring to its highest point (A) and then begins to travel back towards its place of origin. At which point (A, B or C) will the ball travel to after it hits the spring a second time?

A   B   C

11. Which of the two boulders of equal weight (A or B) requires more force to push up the same length of hill? (If equal, mark C)

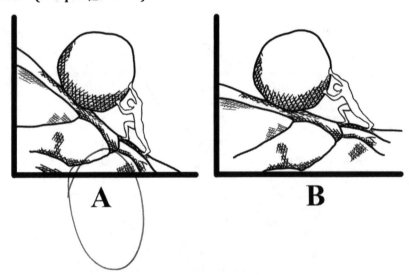

A   B

12. At which point (A, B or C) will the cannonball be traveling the slowest?

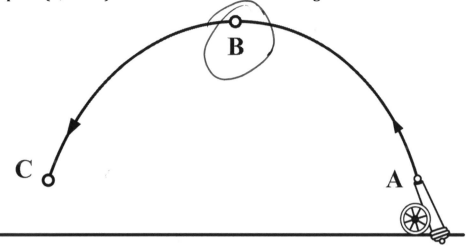

13. On which side of the pipe (A or B) would the water speed be slower? (If equal, mark C)

14. In which of the two figures (A or B) is the person bearing more weight? (If equal, mark C)

15. Which of the two lift trucks (A or B) carrying the same amount of weight is more likely to tip over? (If equal, mark C)

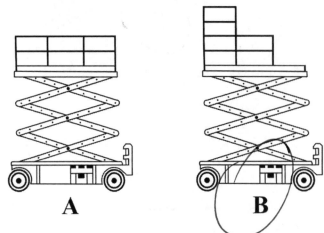

16. The weight of the boxes is being carried by the two men shown below. Which of the two men (A or B) is carrying more weight? (If equal, mark C)

17. In the pictures below, which of the angles (A or B) is braced more solidly? (If equal, mark C)

higher on post

18. Given two birds sitting on branches of a tree at different elevations. Both drop objects of identical size and weight. Which object (A or B) will hit the ground with bigger force? (If equal, mark C)

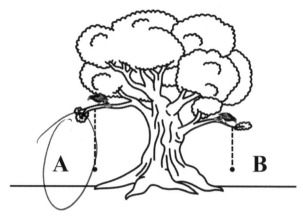

19. A wagon is pulled up two hills of equal slope and height. For which hill (A or B) did the wagon require less effort to reach the top? (If equal, mark C)

20. In which of the three positions (A, B or C) will it be easiest to accurately measure the amount of liquid in the graduated cylinder?

21. In which of the two figures (A or B) will the person require less force to lift a 100-pound weight? (If equal, mark C)

97

22. Which switch (A, B or C) should be closed to give power to the light?

C creates a closed loop from one terminal of the battery through the light and back to the other terminal.

23. If the baseball and bowling ball are moving at the same speed, in which direction will the bowling ball tend to go when it collides with the baseball at point X?

Big dog

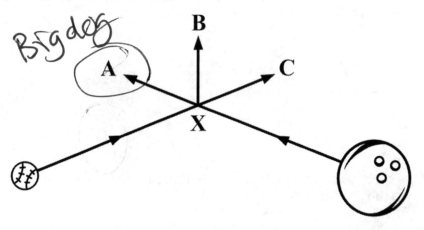

24. Which of the two rolls of paper towels (A or B) will undergo more revolutions if the ends of each roll were pulled downward with the same amount of force? (If equal, mark C)

A   B

98

25. In which of the two containers (A or B) will water that is boiled to the same temperature cool more slowly? (If equal, mark C)

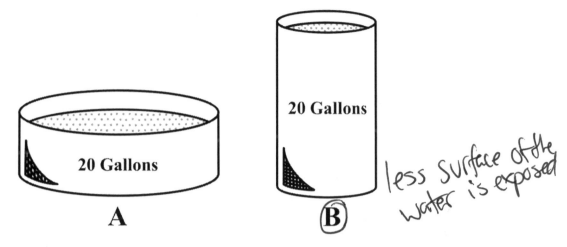

less Surface of the water is exposed

26. Salt is mixed into the water inside container A until it reaches a 50% solution. No salt is added to the water in container B. In which of the two containers (A or B) is an egg more likely to float? (If equal, mark C)

Salt increases density of solution

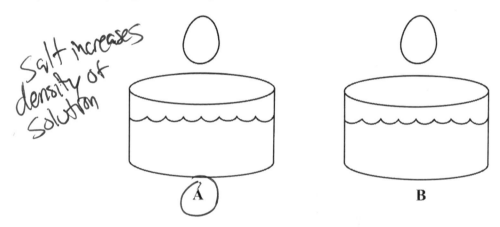

27. Which reflector (A or B) on the bicycle wheel is going to be traveling a greater distance when the wheel turns? (If equal, mark C)

28. A javelin is thrown into the air. At which point (A, B or C) will the javelin be traveling the fastest?

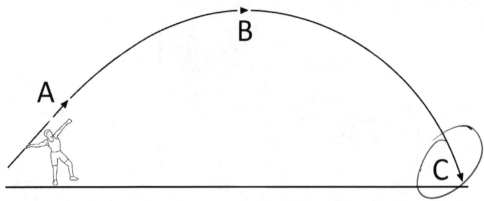

29. A child is released on the seat of a swing set at the position shown. To which point (A, B or C) will the child travel before he/she begins to return back to the point of origin?

30. On which side of the pipe (A or B) would the water speed be slower? (If equal, mark C)

Equal

31. Given two objects shown below that are dropped from an elevation of 100 feet. Neglecting air resistance, which object (A or B) will fall at a faster rate? (If equal, mark C)

Same rate

A   B

32. An athlete is holding a heavy metal ball attached to a wire and is rotating in the circular motion shown below. In which direction (A, B or C) would the ball travel when it is released at point X?

think like shooting out of a moving barrel

33. Which of the two wheels (A or B) will allow you to travel a further distance given the same rotational speed? (If equal, mark C)

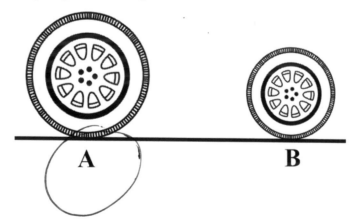

A   B

34. Two tanks with different capacities contain the same amount of gas, 50 kg. In which of the given tanks (A or B) will the gas pressure be greater? (If equal, mark C)

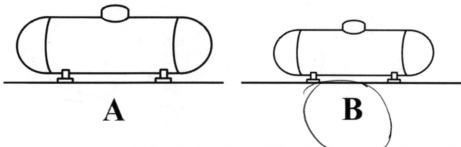

A   **B**

35. Given two water towers with identical tanks and identical amounts of water in each tank, which tower (A or B) will have greater water pressure coming out of the hose? Tank A is 80 feet tall and tank B is 180 feet tall. (If equal, mark C)

80 Feet   180 Feet

36. The weight of the boxes is resting on a platform suspended in the air by two ropes. Which of the two ropes (A or B) is supporting more of the weight? (If equal, mark C)

A   B

37. Container A contains 100 mL pure water and container B contains 100 mL oil. Assume two identical objects are thrown into the two containers; in which of these two containers is the object more likely to float? (If equally likely, mark C)

A   B

38. Which of the two scenarios (A or B) requires less effort to pull the weight up off the ground? (If equal, mark C)

A   B

39. It takes a ball 1.25 seconds to reach the bottom of ramp A and 2.50 seconds to reach the bottom of ramp B. For which ramp (A or B) does the ball have more potential energy? (If equal, mark C)

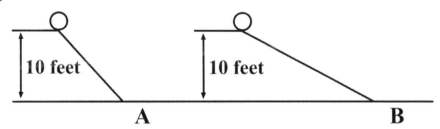

10 feet   10 feet

A   B

103

40. Container A holds 1 qt of water and container B holds 1 qt of motor oil. Assume each container is poured down a funnel at the same time. Which of the two contents will reach the bottom of the funnel more quickly? (If equal, mark C)

41. A full goblet is attached to the inside of a wheel rotating at a rate of 30 revolutions per second. In which direction (A or B) will the contents of the glass tend to go as the wheel rotates? (If none, mark C)

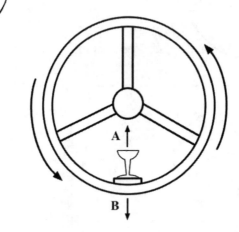

42. Which car (A or B) will travel a greater distance on the given track? (If equal, mark C)

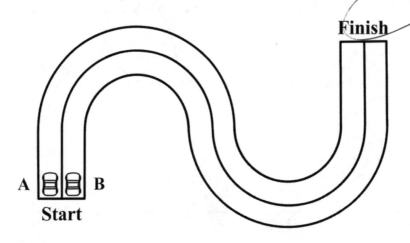

43. In which direction (A or B) will the ball move once the sticks of dynamite explode? (If neither, mark C)

44. In which direction (A or B) will pulley 4 spin if pulley 1 is spinning counter-clockwise? (If none, mark C)

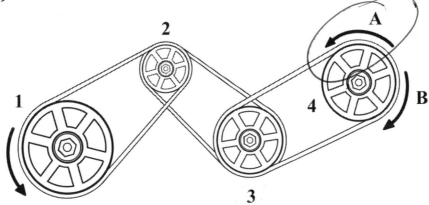

Graphic Arithmetic

Questions 1-8 pertain to the following figure:

Figure 1. Office Building Floor Plan

1. What is the distance ("A") from the left edge of the property to the break room?

a. 47'
b. 67'
c. 70'
d. 19'
e. N

2. What is the distance ("B") from the top edge of the property to the conference room?

a. 57'
b. 22'
c. 27'
d. 59'
e. N

3. What is the distance ("C") from the bottom of the property to the employee office?

   a. 19'
   b. 60'
   c. 10'
   d. 18'
   e. N

4. What is the area of the manager's office?

   a. 44 ft²

   b. 480 ft²
   c. 360 ft²
   d. 576 ft²
   e. N

5. How much wider (top to bottom) is the conference room than the break room?

   a. 7'
   b. 23'
   c. 27'

   d. 4'
   e. N

6. The total width (left to right) of the property is ___ times wider than the administrative assistant's office.

   a. 6.5
   b. 6.2
   c. 5.5
   d. 5.8
   e. N

7. What is the total perimeter of the property?

   a. 196'
   b. 468'

   c. 392'
   d. 316'
   e. N

8. What is the length ("E") of the custodian's office?

   a. 16'

   b. 13'
   c. 11'
   d. 12'
   e. N

Questions 9-16 pertain to the following figure:

Figure 2. Electrical Panel

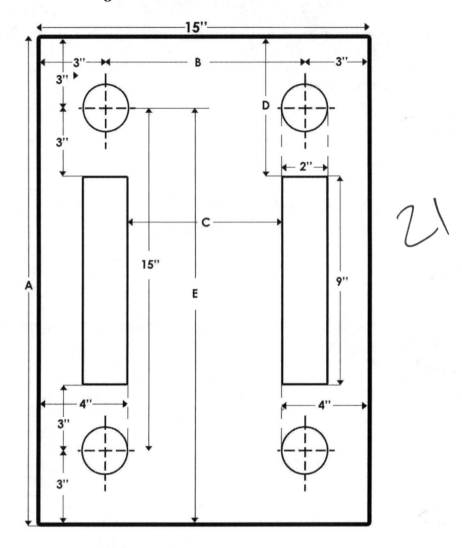

9. What is the length ("A") of the electrical panel?

    a. 18"
    b. 21"
    c. 22"
    d. 15"
    e. N

10. What is the width ("B") between the centers of the top two holes?

    a. 10"
    b. 8"
    c. 15"
    d. 9"
    e. N

11. What is the area of one of the rectangular cutouts?
    a. 81 sq. in.
    b. 21 sq. in.
    c. 18 sq. in.
    d. 16 sq. in.
    e. N

12. What is the distance ("C") between the two rectangular cutouts?
    a. 8"
    b. 7"
    c. 9"
    d. 7.5"
    e. N

13. What is the diameter of the drilled holes?
    a. 2"
    b. 3"
    c. 4"
    d. 1"
    e. N

14. What is the distance ("D") from the top of the panel to the top of the rectangular opening?
    a. 5"
    b. 9"
    c. 3"
    d. 6"
    e. N

15. What is the distance ("E") from the center of the top holes to the bottom of the panel?
    a. 21"
    b. 19"
    c. 18"
    d. 17"
    e. N

16. What is the total perimeter of the panel?
    a. 72"
    b. 60"
    c. 62"
    d. 84"
    e. N

Reading for Comprehension

Passage #1

A hydroelectric power plant uses the potential energy of water to generate electricity. These facilities must be located next to a large body of water, whether natural or man-made. The amount of energy that can be developed by the plant is directly proportional to the volume of water at the site, as well as the rate at which the water is allowed to flow through the plant. In a typical arrangement, the power plant is built atop or alongside a dam, through which water is permitted to flow at a controlled pace. This water flow spins turbines that are attached to alternators, which generate the electrical power.

Hydroelectric power plants have many wonderful qualities relative to other plants. They are very clean and are inexpensive to operate and maintain. Hydroelectric plants are also very reliable and can move from inaction to operation at full capacity in a matter of minutes. These plants can be operated with a great deal of precision, which promotes efficiency. Finally, hydroelectric plants are considered to be one of the most durable systems, which means that they maintain their efficiency throughout their lives.

Unfortunately, hydroelectric power plants have specific demands that can be difficult to meet. They require a long area, and they cost a great deal of money to construct. They also tend to have long transmission lines, so they are subject to a number of inefficiencies. Perhaps the most negative aspect of a hydroelectric power plant is not associated with the plant itself, but with the large reservoir of water that must be alongside the plant. These reservoirs submerge huge amounts of land and can have devastating effects on wildlife and human settlements alike. Moreover, hydroelectric power plants are dependent on the water supply, so prolonged droughts can make it impossible for these facilities to operate.

Clearly, hydroelectric power plants cannot be built just anywhere. The best sites for these plants are large lakes at high altitude, especially in areas that receive a great deal of rainfall. It is good for the land to be rocky, because this will make it better able to support the heavy equipment that must be used in construction and operation. Also, it is important for there to be adequate roads or rails to move all of this equipment. All of these requirements mean that only a few sites will be truly appropriate for a hydroelectric power plant.

1. Which phrase from the passage best illustrates that a hydroelectric plant should be placed next to a large body of water?

    a. "The amount of energy that can be developed by the plant is directly proportional to the volume of water at the site."

    b. "These reservoirs submerge huge amounts of land and can have devastating effects on wildlife and human settlements alike."

    c. "In a typical arrangement, the power plant is built atop or alongside a dam, through which water is permitted to flow at a controlled pace."

    d. "Hydroelectric power plants are dependent on the water supply."

2. In a hydroelectric power plant, what do the alternators do?

    a. cool the water

    b. generate the electrical power

    c. maintain efficiency

    d. spin the turbines

3. Which of the following is NOT an advantage of hydroelectric power plants?
a. They are clean
b. They are inexpensive to operate
c. They are durable
d. They are inexpensive to construct

4. What does it mean in the second paragraph when it says that "Hydroelectric power plants have many wonderful qualities relative to other plants"?
a. Hydroelectric power plants have many similarities with other plants.
b. Hydroelectric power plants have many advantages over other plants.
c. Hydroelectric power plants have many disadvantages compared to other plants.
d. Hydroelectric power plants have many differences from other plants.

5. Based on the information in the passage, which of the following is probably true?
a. Most hydroelectric power plants are built on sandy soil.
b. Hydroelectric power plants must be built next to natural bodies of water.
c. Hydroelectric plants are more expensive to operate than nuclear plants.
d. An old hydroelectric power plant is approximately as efficient as a new one.

6. Why is rocky soil better for a hydroelectric power plant?
a. The rocks can be used to build the plant.
b. It is better at supporting heavy equipment.
c. Rocky soil tends to contain less vegetation.
d. Bodies of water are usually surrounded by rocky soil.

7. The last paragraph of the passage deals primarily with
a. the selection of a site for a hydroelectric power plant.
b. the need for rocky soil under a hydroelectric power plant
c. the advantages of hydroelectric power plants
d. the disadvantages of hydroelectric power plants

Passage #2

Nuclear power is produced in reactors. The chain reaction created inside a reactor is an example of controlled fission, because the intensity of the reaction and the amount of energy produced are carefully modulated. The fission in a nuclear reactor is also continuous, which means that there is an ever-present risk of accident. In order for nuclear power plants to function safely, the reactor core must be cooled constantly.

The production of electricity in a nuclear power plant requires sufficient raw material. In most cases, the fuel is a naturally occurring isotope of uranium, U-235. This isotope is fairly common, but for the purpose of nuclear power production it must be present in very large amounts, which requires purification and concentration until at least 3% of the material is U-235. Once enough of this material has been created, the uranium is molded into standardized, consistent units. These are typically cylindrical pellets with a thickness of about a quarter inch and a length of about an inch. Each of these pellets has a mass of only 8.5 grams, yet can produce as much energy as a ton of coal!

After the uranium has been formed into pellets, the pellets are stacked inside four-meter metal rods, which are then bound together to form fuel assemblies, which themselves are bound together inside the reactor core. The reactor core is a heavy steel container. Neutrons are then fired into the reactor core, where they dislodge neutrons from the unstable uranium atoms. Because the uranium is packed so tightly within the reactor core, any neutrons that are knocked loose from one atom go on to dislodge other neutrons from atoms, a chain reaction that enables the release of massive amounts of energy.

The core of a nuclear reactor gets extremely hot, so a coolant is used. Typically, this coolant is water, although breeder reactors, which get much hotter than conventional ones, use liquid sodium. In a breeder reactor, the fission of uranium produces plutonium, which itself can be used as nuclear fuel. The coolant in a nuclear reactor is also useful as a moderator, which means that it slows down the neutrons. This makes it easier to modulate the efficiency of the reactor's operation. Without coolant, the fuel rods in the reactor core may melt, at which point the control rods will not be able to control the reaction. The reactor core may become so hot that it triggers a meltdown, in which the floor beneath the reactor is disintegrated and radioactive material is released into the environment.

8. Which of the following would be the best title for this passage?
   a. "The Production of Nuclear Power"
   b. "Nuclear Waste Disposal"
   c. "The Uses of Uranium"
   d. "Reactors and Coolants"

9. Which of the following statements about the uranium used in nuclear power production is true?
   a. It does not need to be processed before use.
   b. It can be used to produce weapons.
   c. It cannot be purified.
   d. It occurs naturally.

10. Based on the information in the passage, seventeen grams of uranium fuel could produce as much energy as

a. half a ton of coal.
b. a ton of coal.
c. two tons of coal.
d. three tons of coal.

11. According to the passage, why does dislodging one neutron in the reactor core result in a chain reaction?

a. Because the material is radioactive
b. Because it is packed so tightly
c. Because uranium is unstable
d. Because the reactor must be cooled

12. Out of what metal is the reactor core constructed?

a. iron
b. steel
c. uranium
d. plutonium

13. What is the subject of the passage's final paragraph?

a. the cooling of the reactor
b. water
c. how the reactor works
d. nuclear meltdowns

14. What is the typical coolant in a nuclear reactor?

a. water
b. natural gas
c. plutonium
d. liquid sodium

Passage #3

Electricity is an essential part of modern life, but it can be dangerous and even deadly if proper safety procedures are not followed. When the amount of current passing through a wire increases, so does the amount of heat generated. If the wires become too hot, they can start a fire. Therefore, before electricity could be used within the home, there needed to be devices that could diminish, divert, or turn off electrical current. The three most common tools for this purpose are fuses, breakers, and switches.

There are two main types of fuse available for use in homes: the Edison-base fuse and the type S fuse. An Edison-base fuse screws into a socket by means of a threaded, spiraled bottom, much like a lightbulb. This is convenient, but it also makes it very easy to screw the wrong fuse into the socket. If an Edison-base fuse is screwed into a socket that requires a much higher voltage, it will blow immediately. If the fuse is screwed into a socket that requires much lower voltage, it will fail to blow even when dangerous levels of electricity are passing through the wire.

The potential for this error was eliminated with the introduction of the type S fuse, so called because the wire inside the fuse is bent into an S shape. The type S fuse is specially sized and designed so that fuses can only be screwed into the appropriate sockets. Still, fuses are considered too unreliable for use in the home and are used more often in cars these days.

In most homes, electrical safety is provided by a system of circuit breakers. Like a fuse, a circuit contains a bimetallic strip, through which the current passes. As the current increases, the strip begins to bend; if the current becomes too great, the strip will bend too much, and the circuit will be broken.

Of course, in order for a fuse or breaker to be effective, it must be at the right place in the circuit. For instance, many appliances contain a grounding wire, which connects the circuit with the casing (that is, the outside of the appliance). If a hot wire comes into contact with the casing, the current immediately blows the fuse or trips the breaker. In this arrangement, the switch, fuse, or circuit breaker must always be on the high-voltage, rather than the ground, side of the line. If the switch or fuse was placed on the ground side, an open circuit would have no current but would retain a potential current, which a person could complete, at his or her peril, by touching the appliance.

15. What would be the best title for this passage?
a. "Edison-base fuses, type S fuses, circuit breakers, and grounding wires"
b. "Electrical Safety Devices"
c. "Deadly Electricity"
d. "Switches, etc."

16. Which of the following is NOT one of the common devices for maintaining electrical safety?
a. fuse
b. battery
c. switch
d. breaker

17. What is the major problem with the Edison-base fuse?

a. They are no longer manufactured
b. They occasionally explode
c. They are very expensive
d. Every fuse fits into every socket

18. Why does the S type fuse have that name?

a. Because the wire inside is shaped like an S
b. Because it came after the R type fuse
c. Because it requires S type batteries
d. Because it screws into a socket

19. What does a grounding wire connect?

a. the casing and the fuse
b. the circuit and the casing
c. the breaker and the circuit
d. the fuse and the circuit

20. What is the purpose of an Edison-base fuse's threaded bottom?

a. To combine with a grounding wire
b. To indicate the appropriate level of current
c. To improve the efficiency of the fuse
d. To enable the fuse to be screwed into a socket

21. On an electrical appliance, where is the casing?

a. On the outside
b. Underneath
c. Above
d. Behind the electronic display

Passage #4

A modern steam power plant is fairly simple in its operation. In short, a coal fire turns water into steam inside a turbine, and the resulting pressure drives an alternator. The steam is then condensed back into water so that it can be used again. This process seems fairly simple, though in recent decades it has been modified slightly to improve the efficiency of these plants.

In a modern steam power plant, coal arrives by means of road, rail, or water. A series of fuel feeding devices transport the coal to the furnaces, where it is burnt. All of the ash that is produced by the burning of coal will be shunted to the back of the furnace and placed on scrap conveyors, which will then remove the ash to a storage compartment. Modern coal-fired steam power plants have electronic controls that govern the relative amounts of air and coal allowed into the furnace, which moderates the rate of combustion.

Meanwhile, a fan draws air from the outside into the plant, where it is preheated and then further warmed by the flue gases as they pass to the chimney. This air is then sent into the furnace. The preheating of the furnace air improves the efficiency of the plant considerably.

The heat from the furnace converts the water in the turbines to steam, which powers an alternator. After this steam leaves the turbine, it enters a condenser, so that it can be reconverted to water and used again. The modern steam power plant uses a condensate pump to remove the water from the condenser, at which point it enters a low-pressure water heater. This heater receives its warmth from the steam that escapes from the turbine. The water is further reheated in a high-pressure water heater, and then it is pumped into a boiler. Inside the boiler, the water is converted into high-pressure wet steam, where it is heated even further and fed into the turbine.

At the same time, the modern steam power plant will be circulating cool water throughout the facility, but especially around the condenser. This water will be drawn from a nearby natural source, such as a river or lake. The plant will need to use filters to prevent sediment and other particulate matter from damaging the machinery.

22. **What affects the rate of combustion in the furnace?**
   a.   the amount of air only
   b.   the amount of coal only
   c.   both the amount of air and the amount of coal
   d.   neither the amount of air nor the amount of coal

23. **Which of the following would be the best title for this passage?**
   a.   "How a Modern Steam Power Plant Works"
   b.   "The Operation of a Power Plant"
   c.   "I Dream of Steam"
   d.   "The Pros and Cons of Steam Power Plants"

24. **In a modern steam power plant, water is pumped out of the condenser and into a**
   a.   furnace.
   b.   high-pressure heater.
   c.   low-pressure heater.
   d.   turbine.

25. When the passage mentions in the second paragraph that ash will be "shunted," what is the closest synonym?

    a. moved

    b. destroyed

    c. burnt

    d. purchased

26. What is the main purpose of this passage?

    a. To advocate the construction of new steam power plants

    b. To describe how the primary energy source arrives at a steam power plant

    c. To entertain the reader with a story about steam power

    d. To explain the operation of a modern steam power plant

27. Why is cool water circulated around the condenser?

    a. So that the water can be reheated

    b. Because keeping the condenser cool helps it turn the steam back into water

    c. To prevent it from escaping the facility

    d. To power the condenser's operation

28. What is the primary subject of the last paragraph?

    a. the steam that spins the turbines

    b. the water used to cool the plant

    c. the employees of the plant

    d. the water used to spin the turbines

Passage #5

Despite its bad reputation in the United States, nuclear power has some advantages for the environment over other sources of energy. Oil, coal, and natural gas all release carbon dioxide and other gases that contribute to global warming, but nuclear power does not. Moreover, nuclear power plants generate neither sulfur oxides nor nitrogen oxides, so they do not contribute to acid rain.

However, nuclear plants do generate hazardous waste. The rods used for fuel expire and need to be replaced. These rods are extremely radioactive. Moreover, there are thousands of nuclear power plants around the world, so the total amount of high-level nuclear waste is significant. In some countries, such as France, the problem of disposing of this material is solved by reusing it. However, in the United States the breeder reactors that make reuse possible have not been viable at the commercial level, so safely disposing of nuclear waste continues to bedevil politicians, plant owners, and environmentalists.

At present, a number of approaches are used in the United States for the disposal of waste. In over thirty states, high-level nuclear waste is stored in above-ground facilities. However, some groups are beginning to use geologic repository systems, in which the waste is encased in lead or concrete and buried in an underground tunnel. This method of disposal is promising, but it is impossible in areas where earthquakes are likely or where groundwater can seep in.

Another possibility is called subductive waste disposal. This entails attaching or embedding hazardous waste to a tectonic plate that is in the process of sliding underneath another and would therefore carry the waste into the Earth's mantle. This inventive solution would most likely use the tectonic plates at the bottom of the ocean, both because these are out of the way and because they are the plates most actively engaged in subduction. However, the rate at which tectonic plates move is so slow (a few centimeters a year) that subductive waste disposal has largely been dismissed. Even its proponents admit that it would require storage techniques superior to those in use at present.

A final idea focuses on the disposal of weapons-grade plutonium. In what is known as the mixed oxide method, plutonium is mixed with uranium so that it can be used again in nuclear reactors. The waste that would result from this second round of power generation would be hazardous still, but less hazardous than the source plutonium. At the very least, the waste material derived from the mixed oxide method cannot be used in weaponry and is much easier to store.

29. The subject of this passage is

a. subductive waste disposal.
b. nuclear power plants.
c. nuclear waste disposal.
d. nuclear power.

30. Which of the following harmful gases is produced by nuclear power plants?

a. carbon dioxide
b. sulfur dioxide
c. nitrogen dioxide
d. None of the above

31. Which of the following sentences best asserts the main idea of the passage?

    a. "However, nuclear plants do generate hazardous waste."

    b. "Despite its bad reputation in the United States, nuclear power has some advantages for the environment over other sources of energy."

    c. "Oil, coal, and natural gas all release carbon dioxide and other gases that contribute to global warming, but nuclear power does not."

    d. "Moreover, there are thousands of nuclear power plants around the world, so the total amount of high-level nuclear waste is significant."

32. Which of the following statements about nuclear power in the United States is true?

    a. All of the nuclear waste in the United States is disposed of in the same way.

    b. There are a number of active breeder reactors in the United States.

    c. The United States employs several different methods for nuclear waste disposal.

    d. The United States is the only country to use subductive waste disposal techniques.

33. Which method of nuclear waste disposal involves creating a new form of nuclear fuel?

    a. mixed oxide

    b. subductive waste disposal

    c. hazardous waste sequestration

    d. geologic repository

34. When one tectonic plate slides underneath another, it is called

    a. repository.

    b. inferiority.

    c. sequestration.

    d. subduction.

35. What is the main problem with subductive waste disposal?

    a. Tectonic plates move too slowly.

    b. It requires plutonium to be converted into uranium.

    c. Subduction occurs too quickly.

    d. It is susceptible to contamination by groundwater.

36. Which of the following statements about the mixed oxide method is true?

    a. The resulting plutonium can be used in weapons.

    b. It produces waste that is easier to store.

    c. It involves mixing plutonium with thorium.

    d. It requires storage facilities under the sea.

Mathematical Usage

Use the following information to answer questions 1-18:

1 acre =	43,560 square feet
1 barrel =	42 gallons
1 fathom =	6 feet
1 foot =	12 inches
1 furlong =	40 rods
1 gallon =	3.785 liters
1 gallon =	4 quarts
1 hand =	10 centimeters
1 inch =	2.54 centimeters
1 kilogram =	1,000 grams
1 kilogram =	2.2 pounds
1 kilometer =	1,000 meters
1 mile =	1.609 kilometers
1 mile =	5,280 feet
3 mile/hour =	4.4 feet/second
1 pint =	4 gills
1 pound =	16 ounces
1 quart =	2 pints
1 slug =	14.59 kilograms
1 square mile =	640 acres

If none of the answers listed are correct, select answer e, N for none of the above.

1. 6 kilograms = ? pounds

    a. 2.2
    b. 6,000
    c. 15.2
    d. 13.2
    e. N

2. 4 furlongs = ? rods

    a. 160
    b. 10
    c. 40
    d. 0.1
    e. N

3. 80 ounces = ? pounds

a. 5
b. 16
c. 8
d. 10
e. N

4. 3 acres = ? square feet

a. 43,560
b. 1,920
c. 130,680
d. 640
e. N

5. 2 miles = ? kilometers

a. 1.609
b. 3.218
c. 1.243
d. 2.486
e. N

6. 3 quart = ? gallons

a. 0.33
b. 4
c. 1.33
d. 0.75
e. N

7. 12 fathoms = ? feet

a. 2
b. 12
c. 72
d. 6
e. N

8. 126 gallons = ? barrels

a. 3
b. 4
c. 42
d. 5292
e. N

9. **60 miles/hour = ? feet/second**

    a. 5
    b. 100
    c. 41
    d. 88
    e. N

10. **500 grams = ? kilograms**

    a. 500,000
    b. 0.5
    c. 50
    d. 0.05
    e. N

11. **15 hands = ? centimeters**

    a. 38
    b. 1.5
    c. 60
    d. 150
    e. N

12. **15.14 liters = ? gallons**

    a. 2
    b. 3
    c. 4
    d. 5
    e. N

13. **2 barrels = ? quarts**

    a. 336
    b. 21
    c. 168
    d. 672
    e. N

14. **1 mile = ? centimeters**

    a. 849,733,632
    b. 160,934
    c. 13,411
    d. 30.5
    e. N

15. 13.2 pounds = ? grams

- a. 6
- b. 60
- c. 600
- d. 6,000
- e. N

16. 8 fathoms = ? inches

- a. 96
- b. 48
- c. 576
- d. 4,608
- e. N

17. 8 quarts = ? liters

- a. 7.57
- b. 121.12
- c. 15.14
- d. 0.53
- e. N

18. 5 feet = ? centimeters

- a. 12.7
- b. 23.6
- c. 152.4
- d. 60
- e. N

Answer Key and Explanations

Mechanical Concepts

1. B: When an object is submerged into a container of liquid, it naturally displaces an amount of liquid equivalent to that object's volume. Object 2 is larger than object 1, so it will displace a greater volume of water and cause the level in tank B to be higher than that of tank A.

2. A: Newton's third law is used to understand that momentum is conserved in all collisions, and there is no indication that the balls merge into one upon colliding. Because of this, the balls will conserve momentum but exchange direction with the ball they collide with. In this case, ball 1 will rebound off ball 2 in the direction ball 2 was initially traveling; i.e., toward the upper left pocket (A). Conversely, ball 2 will follow ball 1's initial path toward the upper right pocket.

3. A: Consecutively attached gears alternate rotation direction, which means all even-numbered gears will turn in one corresponding direction, and all odd-numbered gears will turn the opposite corresponding direction. Since gear 1 is spinning counter-clockwise, all other odd-numbered gears will spin counter-clockwise as well (A). Gears 2 and 4 will spin clockwise.

4. B: The spring under object B is compressed noticeably further, and therefore has more elastic potential energy stored up to launch the ball higher into the air.

5. B: Water (along with nearly every other substance) seeks the lowest energy state in which to rest. Functionally, this means that the water level will be equally high in all parts of the watering can.

6. C: Every point on the belt, and consequently every point on the outside of each pulley, is moving at the same linear speed. Therefore, the pulley with the smallest circumference will rotate the fastest.

7. B: A pulley only reduces the amount of force required to lift an object if the weight is distributed across multiple sections of the rope, as is done in A. The force needed to pull the weight is reduced, but the distance the rope must be pulled increases in proportion to the number of pulleys used.

8. C: Only switch C creates a closed loop between the generator and the motor. Closing B creates a short circuit that does not pass through the motor, and closing A does nothing.

9. A: The mechanical advantage of an inclined plane can be determined by dividing the length by the height. Since both ramps are 5 feet tall, the mechanical advantage of ramp A is significantly lower at 4. As mechanical advantage decreases, the amount of force needed increases proportionally, so ramp A will require much more force.

10. B: Because of friction losses within the spring and between the ball and the surface, the ball will not travel as far the second time.

11. A: More force is required to push a boulder up a steeper incline because it has less mechanical advantage.

12. B: In ballistic flight, the horizontal component of velocity is essentially constant. At point B, the vertical component of the cannonball's velocity is zero, making the peak of its arc the slowest point.

124

13. A: Since the same volume of water that enters the pipe must exit as well, the water must travel significantly faster at point B to move the same volume, since the opening is much smaller. In other words, as the cross-sectional area of a pipe decreases, the speed of the water must increase to maintain the same volume flow rate.

14. A: In figure A, the load is centered much closer to the man and much farther from the wheel (fulcrum) than in figure B. This means that the man will have to bear a larger percentage of the weight of the load.

15. B: On truck A, the load is evenly distributed, while on truck B it is concentrated on one end, making it more likely to tip over.

16. B: The load on the stretcher is concentrated more closely to man B than man A, so man B is bearing more of the load.

17. A: The bracing in A is more solid because it extends higher up on the post.

18. A: Though the force of gravity is the same on both objects, object A will have had more time to build up speed, so it will hit the ground with more force than object B.

19. B: The wagon will roll more easily up the smoother slope because there is less rolling resistance.

20. C: The amount of liquid will be easiest to measure when the angle of the water line matches the lines drawn on the cylinder.

21. A: In figure A, the weight is much closer to the fulcrum, so it will require less force to raise.

22. C: Only switch C creates a closed loop from one terminal of the battery, through the light, and back to the other terminal.

23. A: Since a bowling ball weighs nearly 50 times as much as a baseball, the bowling ball's path will not be significantly affected by its collision with the baseball, so it will maintain its original trajectory.

24. B: Roll B will turn faster, both because it is lighter, thus having a lower moment of inertia, and because it requires less paper to be pulled to undergo a revolution.

25. B: Water in container B will cool more slowly because less of the surface of the water is exposed to the air.

26. A: Adding salt to water increases the density of the solution, making objects more likely to float on it.

27. A: Reflector A is farther from the center of the wheel. Therefore, it will travel more distance when the wheel turns.

28. C: Since air resistance on a javelin is negligible, and its horizontal velocity is effectively constant throughout its flight, the fastest point will be the point that has the greatest vertical velocity. Since point C is the lowest point, it is the point at which the maximum potential energy will have been converted to kinetic energy.

29. C: The child will travel to the approximately equivalent height on the other side of the swing set before returning to the initial side, as this is simple harmonic motion.

30. C: To maintain a constant volume flow rate, all the water must leave at the same rate at which it enters. Since both the entry and exit pipes have the same size, the water must be traveling at the same speed in both locations.

31. C: In the absence of air resistance, the acceleration of an object in freefall is entirely dependent on gravity and independent of the object's size, shape, or mass. Thus, both objects will fall at the same rate.

32. A: When the ball is released, it will continue traveling in whatever linear direction it was traveling at the time of release. The path it takes will be along a line that is tangent to the circle.

33. A: Since wheel A has a larger circumference, it travels farther on each full rotation.

34. B: The same amount of gas will be under greater pressure in the smaller tank since there is less volume for it to occupy.

35. B: Tank B is 100 feet higher than tank A, which means that the water it holds has an additional 100 feet of potential energy contributing to the pressure at the end of the hose.

36. C: Since the boxes are evenly distributed and their center is equal distance from both ropes, the two ropes support equal amounts of the weight.

37. A: Water is significantly more dense than oil, so an object dropped in water is more likely to float than an identical object dropped in oil.

38. B: In figure A, the weight is split between two sections of the rope, while in figure B, it is distributed among three sections. This means that it will only require a third of the effort to lift the weight in figure B, versus half the weight in figure A.

39. C: Potential energy is dependent on the height of an object relative to the ground. Both ramps are 10 feet tall, so the ball has the same amount of potential energy.

40. A: Oil is much more viscous than water, so it will take longer to reach the bottom of the funnel.

41. C: Since the wheel is rotating so quickly, the contents of the goblet will remain in place because of inertia and centripetal force.

42. C: Both paths are the same length. The first half of path A is identical to the second half of path B, and vice versa.

43. A: The force of the explosion will propel everything above it into the air.

44. A: Because these pulleys are connected by belts, they will all turn in the same direction.

Mometrix

Graphic Arithmetic

1. C: 70'. To find the unknown distance ("A"), subtract the known widths from the total width of the property. The total width of the property is 117'. The other known widths are 20' and 27'. To find A, subtract 20' and 27' from 117'. A + 20' + 27' = 117'. A = 117' - 20' - 27' = 70'.

2. B: 22'. To find the unknown length ("B"), subtract the known lengths from the total length of the property. The total length of the property is 79'. The known lengths are 37' and 20'. To find B, subtract 37' and 20' from 79'. B + 20' + 37' = 79'. B = 79' - 20' - 37' = 22'.

3. A: 19'. To find the unknown length ("C"), subtract the known lengths from the total length of the property. The total length of the property is 79'. The known lengths are 18', 18', and 24'. To find C, subtract 18', 18', and 24' from 79'. C + 18' + 18' + 24' = 79'. C = 79' - 18' - 18' - 24' = 19'.

4. B: 480 ft². To find the area of the manager's office, multiply the length of the office by the width of the office. The length of the office is 24'. The width of the office is 20'. Area of the manager's office = 24' × 20' = 480 ft².

5. D: 4'. The width of the conference room is 20'. The width of the break room is 16'. To find how much wider the conference room is than the break room, subtract the width of the break room from the width of the conference room. 20' - 16' = 4'.

6. A: 6.5. To find the answer, divide the total width by the width of the secretary's office. The width of the total property is 117' and the width of the secretary's office is 18'. 117 ÷ 18 = 6.5

7. C: 392'. To find the perimeter of the property, add all four sides of the property together. Because the property is a rectangle, the width is the same on the top and the bottom, 117'. The length is the same on the right and left, 79'. The total perimeter of the property = 117' + 117' + 79' + 79' = 392'.

8. B: 13'. To find the length of the custodian's office ("E"), subtract the known lengths from the total length of the property. The total length of the property is 79'. The known lengths are 37' and 29'. To find D, subtract 37' and 29' from 79'. D + 37' + 29' = 79'. D = 79' - 37' - 29' = 13'.

9. B: 21". The total length of the panel is found by adding the given lengths of the panel, 3", 15", and 3". A = 3" + 15" + 3" = 21".

10. D: 9". The unknown distance between the two holes is found by subtracting the known distances from the centers of the holes to the edge of the panel from the total width of the panel. 15" = 3" + B + 3". B = 15" - 3" - 3" = 9".

11. C: 18 sq. in. The area of the rectangular cut out is found by the following formula: A = l × w, where A = area, l = length, w = width. The length and width of the rectangular cutouts are given in the drawing as l = 9" and w = 2". Therefore, A = 9" × 2" = 18 sq. in.

12. B: 7". The distance from the edges of the panels to the inside edges of the rectangular cutouts are given to be 4". To find the distance between the panels, subtract these given measurements from the given width of the panels. 15" = 4" + C + 4". C = 15" - 4" - 4" = 7".

13. A: 2". The diameter of a circle is the distance across the circle through the center. This distance is given in the drawing as 2".

14. D: 6". The distance from the top of the panel to the center of the top holes is given in the drawing to be 3". The distance from the center of the top hole to the top of the rectangular opening

127

is given to be 3". To find the total distance from the top of the panel to the top of the rectangular opening, add these distances together. D = 3" + 3" = 6".

15. C: 18". The distance from the center of the top hole to the center of the bottom hole is given in the drawing to be 15". The distance from the center of the bottom hole to the bottom edge of the panel is given to be 3". To find the total distance, add these distances together. E = 15" + 3" = 18".

16. A: 72". The total perimeter of the panel is found by adding the distance of all four sides together. The width of the panel is given in the drawing to be 15". The length of the panel is found to be 21" by adding the given lengths (3" + 15" + 3"). Perimeter = 15" + 15" + 21" + 21" = 72".

Reading for Comprehension

1. A: This information is supplied in the last sentence of the first paragraph.

2. B: This is stated in the last sentence of the first paragraph.

3. D: The second sentence of the third paragraph states that hydroelectric power plants "cost a great deal of money to construct."

4. B: This sentence means that when hydroelectric power plants are compared with other power plants, the hydroelectric plants are found to have many superior qualities.

5. D: This can be inferred from the last sentence of the second paragraph, where it states that "hydroelectric plants are considered to be one of the most durable systems, which means that they maintain their efficiency throughout their lives."

6. B: The third sentence of the last paragraph states that, if the land is rocky, this "will make it better able to support the heavy equipment that must be used in construction and operation."

7. A: The last paragraph of the passage deals primarily with the selection of a site for a hydroelectric power plant, as indicated by the first sentence: "Clearly, hydroelectric power plants cannot be built just anywhere."

8. A: The passage is a general description of the operations in a nuclear reactor, ranging from the required fuel to the use of coolant.

9. D: This information is given in the second sentence of the second paragraph.

10. C: The second paragraph describes the uranium used to fuel a nuclear reactor and then mentions that, "Each of these [uranium] pellets has a mass of only 8.5 grams, yet can produce as much energy as a ton of coal!" Therefore, twice this amount of uranium should produce as much energy as two tons of coal.

11. B: In the fourth sentence of the third paragraph, it states that, "Because the uranium is packed so tightly within the reactor core, any neutrons that are knocked loose from one atom go on to dislodge other neutrons from atoms."

12. B: This information is given in the second sentence of the third paragraph.

13. A: The final paragraph discusses the need for coolant, the types of coolant used, and the catastrophic consequences of a lack of coolant.

14. A: This information is given in the second sentence of the last paragraph.

15. B: The passage discusses the various pieces of equipment used to make electricity safe.

16. B: The opening paragraph describes the importance of electrical safety and then, in the final sentence, states that "The three most common tools for this purpose are fuses, breakers, and switches."

17. D: The third sentence of the second paragraph refers to this problem, mentioning that it "makes it very easy to screw the wrong fuse into the socket." The rest of the second paragraph describes why this can be a dangerous mistake.

18. A: This is indicated in the first sentence of the third paragraph, which states that "so called because the wire inside the fuse is bent into an S shape."

19. B: The second sentence of the last paragraph states that a grounding wire "connects the circuit with the casing."

20. D: In the second sentence of the second paragraph, the passage states that "An Edison-base fuse screws into a socket by means of a threaded, spiraled bottom."

21. A: Within the parentheses in the second sentence of the last paragraph, the passage defines the casing as "the outside of the appliance."

22. C: This information is in the last sentence of the second paragraph.

23. A: The best title for this passage would be "How a Modern Steam Power Plant Works." The passage is entirely about the steps in the operation of a modern steam power plant. The answer choice "The Operation of a Power Plant," is not bad, but it is not as good as the correct choice because it does not identify the specific type of power plant discussed in the passage.

24. C: This information is in the third sentence of the fourth paragraph.

25. A: The passage says that ash is "shunted to the back of the furnace," meaning that it is moved there.

26. D: This is clear from the first sentence of the passage, "A modern steam power plant is fairly simple in its operation."

27. B: The first sentence of the last paragraph mentions that cool water is circulated "throughout the facility, but especially around the condenser." The second sentence of the fourth paragraph describes how a steam power plant uses condensers to turn steam back into water.

28. B: The last paragraph discusses how cool water is circulated through a steam power plant to cool the equipment, in particular the condenser.

29. C: The passage begins by describing the origins of nuclear waste and then details some possible solutions to this problem.

30. D: This information is given in the second and third sentences of the third paragraph.

31. A: The focus of the article is nuclear waste and its disposal.

32. C: This is stated in the first sentence of the third paragraph.

33. A: The final paragraph describes the mixed-oxide method, in which weapons-grade plutonium is mixed with uranium.

34. D: Subduction is never directly defined, but its meaning may be inferred from the context of the fourth paragraph.

35. A: The fourth paragraph of this passage describes subductive waste disposal. In the second-to-last sentence, it states that "the rate at which tectonic plates move is so slow (a few centimeters a year) that subductive waste disposal has largely been dismissed."

36. B: The mixed oxide method is discussed in the final paragraph of the passage.

Mathematical Usage

1. D: 13.2 pounds

$$6 \text{ kilograms} \times \frac{2.2 \text{ pounds}}{1 \text{ kilogram}} = 13.2 \text{ pounds}$$

2. A: 160 rods

$$4 \text{ furlongs} \times \frac{40 \text{ rods}}{1 \text{ furlong}} = 160 \text{ rods}$$

3. A: 5 pounds

$$80 \text{ ounces} \times \frac{1 \text{ pound}}{16 \text{ ounces}} = 5 \text{ pounds}$$

4. C: 130,680 square feet

$$3 \text{ acres} \times \frac{43,560 \text{ sq ft}}{1 \text{ acre}} = 130,680 \text{ sq ft}$$

5. B: 3.218 kilometers

$$2 \text{ miles} \times \frac{1.609 \text{ kilometers}}{1 \text{ mile}} = 3.218 \text{ kilometers}$$

6. D: 0.75 gallons

$$3 \text{ quarts} \times \frac{1 \text{ gallon}}{4 \text{ quarts}} = 0.75 \text{ gallons}$$

7. C: 72 feet

$$12 \text{ fathoms} \times \frac{6 \text{ feet}}{1 \text{ fathom}} = 72 \text{ feet}$$

8. A: 3 barrels

$$126 \text{ gallons} \times \frac{1 \text{ barrel}}{42 \text{ gallons}} = 3 \text{ barrels}$$

9. D: 88 feet/sec

$$60 \frac{\text{miles}}{\text{hr}} \times \frac{4.4 \frac{\text{feet}}{\text{sec}}}{3 \frac{\text{mile}}{\text{hr}}} = 88 \frac{\text{feet}}{\text{sec}}$$

10. B: 0.5 kilograms

$$500 \text{ grams} \times \frac{1 \text{ kilogram}}{1000 \text{ grams}} = 0.5 \text{ kilograms}$$

11. D: 150 centimeters

$$15 \text{ hands} \times \frac{10 \text{ centimeters}}{1 \text{ hand}} = 150 \text{ centimeters}$$

12. C: 4 gallons

$$15.14 \text{ liters} \times \frac{1 \text{ gallon}}{3.785 \text{ liters}} = 4 \text{ gallons}$$

13. A: 336 quarts

$$2 \text{ barrels} \times \frac{42 \text{ gallons}}{1 \text{ barrel}} \times \frac{4 \text{ quarts}}{1 \text{ gallon}} = 336 \text{ quarts}$$

14. B: 160,934 centimeters

$$1 \text{ mile} \times \frac{5280 \text{ feet}}{1 \text{ mile}} \times \frac{12 \text{ inches}}{1 \text{ foot}} \times \frac{2.54 \text{ centimeters}}{1 \text{ inch}} = 160,934 \text{ centimeters}$$

Or, approximately:

$$1 \text{ mile} \times \frac{1.609 \text{ kilometers}}{1 \text{ mile}} \times \frac{100,000 \text{ centimeters}}{1 \text{ kilometer}} = 160,900 \text{ centimeters}$$

15. D: 6000 grams

$$13.2 \text{ pounds} \times \frac{1 \text{ kilogram}}{2.2 \text{ pounds}} \times \frac{1000 \text{ grams}}{1 \text{ kilogram}} = 6000 \text{ grams}$$

16. C: 576 inches

$$8 \text{ fathoms} \times \frac{6 \text{ feet}}{1 \text{ fathom}} \times \frac{12 \text{ inches}}{1 \text{ foot}} = 576 \text{ inches}$$

17. A: 7.57 liters

$$8 \text{ quarts} \times \frac{1 \text{ gallon}}{4 \text{ quarts}} \times \frac{3.785 \text{ quarts}}{1 \text{ gallon}} = 7.57 \text{ liters}$$

18. C: 152.4 centimeters

$$5 \text{ feet} \times \frac{12 \text{ inches}}{1 \text{ foot}} \times \frac{2.54 \text{ centimeters}}{1 \text{ inch}} = 152.4 \text{ centimeters}$$

How to Overcome Test Anxiety

Just the thought of taking a test is enough to make most people a little nervous. A test is an important event that can have a long-term impact on your future, so it's important to take it seriously and it's natural to feel anxious about performing well. But just because anxiety is normal, that doesn't mean that it's helpful in test taking, or that you should simply accept it as part of your life. Anxiety can have a variety of effects. These effects can be mild, like making you feel slightly nervous, or severe, like blocking your ability to focus or remember even a simple detail.

If you experience test anxiety—whether severe or mild—it's important to know how to beat it. To discover this, first you need to understand what causes test anxiety.

Causes of Test Anxiety

While we often think of anxiety as an uncontrollable emotional state, it can actually be caused by simple, practical things. One of the most common causes of test anxiety is that a person does not feel adequately prepared for their test. This feeling can be the result of many different issues such as poor study habits or lack of organization, but the most common culprit is time management. Starting to study too late, failing to organize your study time to cover all of the material, or being distracted while you study will mean that you're not well prepared for the test. This may lead to cramming the night before, which will cause you to be physically and mentally exhausted for the test. Poor time management also contributes to feelings of stress, fear, and hopelessness as you realize you are not well prepared but don't know what to do about it.

Other times, test anxiety is not related to your preparation for the test but comes from unresolved fear. This may be a past failure on a test, or poor performance on tests in general. It may come from comparing yourself to others who seem to be performing better or from the stress of living up to expectations. Anxiety may be driven by fears of the future—how failure on this test would affect your educational and career goals. These fears are often completely irrational, but they can still negatively impact your test performance.

Elements of Test Anxiety

As mentioned earlier, test anxiety is considered to be an emotional state, but it has physical and mental components as well. Sometimes you may not even realize that you are suffering from test anxiety until you notice the physical symptoms. These can include trembling hands, rapid heartbeat, sweating, nausea, and tense muscles. Extreme anxiety may lead to fainting or vomiting. Obviously, any of these symptoms can have a negative impact on testing. It is important to recognize them as soon as they begin to occur so that you can address the problem before it damages your performance.

The mental components of test anxiety include trouble focusing and inability to remember learned information. During a test, your mind is on high alert, which can help you recall information and stay focused for an extended period of time. However, anxiety interferes with your mind's natural processes, causing you to blank out, even on the questions you know well. The strain of testing during anxiety makes it difficult to stay focused, especially on a test that may take several hours. Extreme anxiety can take a huge mental toll, making it difficult not only to recall test information but even to understand the test questions or pull your thoughts together.

133

Effects of Test Anxiety

Test anxiety is like a disease—if left untreated, it will get progressively worse. Anxiety leads to poor performance, and this reinforces the feelings of fear and failure, which in turn lead to poor performances on subsequent tests. It can grow from a mild nervousness to a crippling condition. If allowed to progress, test anxiety can have a big impact on your schooling, and consequently on your future.

Test anxiety can spread to other parts of your life. Anxiety on tests can become anxiety in any stressful situation, and blanking on a test can turn into panicking in a job situation. But fortunately, you don't have to let anxiety rule your testing and determine your grades. There are a number of relatively simple steps you can take to move past anxiety and function normally on a test and in the rest of life.

Physical Steps for Beating Test Anxiety

While test anxiety is a serious problem, the good news is that it can be overcome. It doesn't have to control your ability to think and remember information. While it may take time, you can begin taking steps today to beat anxiety.

Just as your first hint that you may be struggling with anxiety comes from the physical symptoms, the first step to treating it is also physical. Rest is crucial for having a clear, strong mind. If you are tired, it is much easier to give in to anxiety. But if you establish good sleep habits, your body and mind will be ready to perform optimally, without the strain of exhaustion. Additionally, sleeping well helps you to retain information better, so you're more likely to recall the answers when you see the test questions.

Getting good sleep means more than going to bed on time. It's important to allow your brain time to relax. Take study breaks from time to time so it doesn't get overworked, and don't study right before bed. Take time to rest your mind before trying to rest your body, or you may find it difficult to fall asleep.

Along with sleep, other aspects of physical health are important in preparing for a test. Good nutrition is vital for good brain function. Sugary foods and drinks may give a burst of energy but this burst is followed by a crash, both physically and emotionally. Instead, fuel your body with protein and vitamin-rich foods.

Also, drink plenty of water. Dehydration can lead to headaches and exhaustion, especially if your brain is already under stress from the rigors of the test. Particularly if your test is a long one, drink water during the breaks. And if possible, take an energy-boosting snack to eat between sections.

Along with sleep and diet, a third important part of physical health is exercise. Maintaining a steady workout schedule is helpful, but even taking 5-minute study breaks to walk can help get your blood pumping faster and clear your head. Exercise also releases endorphins, which contribute to a positive feeling and can help combat test anxiety.

When you nurture your physical health, you are also contributing to your mental health. If your body is healthy, your mind is much more likely to be healthy as well. So take time to rest, nourish your body with healthy food and water, and get moving as much as possible. Taking these physical steps will make you stronger and more able to take the mental steps necessary to overcome test anxiety.

Mental Steps for Beating Test Anxiety

Working on the mental side of test anxiety can be more challenging, but as with the physical side, there are clear steps you can take to overcome it. As mentioned earlier, test anxiety often stems from lack of preparation, so the obvious solution is to prepare for the test. Effective studying may be the most important weapon you have for beating test anxiety, but you can and should employ several other mental tools to combat fear.

First, boost your confidence by reminding yourself of past success—tests or projects that you aced. If you're putting as much effort into preparing for this test as you did for those, there's no reason you should expect to fail here. Work hard to prepare; then trust your preparation.

Second, surround yourself with encouraging people. It can be helpful to find a study group, but be sure that the people you're around will encourage a positive attitude. If you spend time with others who are anxious or cynical, this will only contribute to your own anxiety. Look for others who are motivated to study hard from a desire to succeed, not from a fear of failure.

Third, reward yourself. A test is physically and mentally tiring, even without anxiety, and it can be helpful to have something to look forward to. Plan an activity following the test, regardless of the outcome, such as going to a movie or getting ice cream.

When you are taking the test, if you find yourself beginning to feel anxious, remind yourself that you know the material. Visualize successfully completing the test. Then take a few deep, relaxing breaths and return to it. Work through the questions carefully but with confidence, knowing that you are capable of succeeding.

Developing a healthy mental approach to test taking will also aid in other areas of life. Test anxiety affects more than just the actual test—it can be damaging to your mental health and even contribute to depression. It's important to beat test anxiety before it becomes a problem for more than testing.

Study Strategy

Being prepared for the test is necessary to combat anxiety, but what does being prepared look like? You may study for hours on end and still not feel prepared. What you need is a strategy for test prep. The next few pages outline our recommended steps to help you plan out and conquer the challenge of preparation.

STEP 1: SCOPE OUT THE TEST

Learn everything you can about the format (multiple choice, essay, etc.) and what will be on the test. Gather any study materials, course outlines, or sample exams that may be available. Not only will this help you to prepare, but knowing what to expect can help to alleviate test anxiety.

STEP 2: MAP OUT THE MATERIAL

Look through the textbook or study guide and make note of how many chapters or sections it has. Then divide these over the time you have. For example, if a book has 15 chapters and you have five days to study, you need to cover three chapters each day. Even better, if you have the time, leave an extra day at the end for overall review after you have gone through the material in depth.

If time is limited, you may need to prioritize the material. Look through it and make note of which sections you think you already have a good grasp on, and which need review. While you are studying, skim quickly through the familiar sections and take more time on the challenging parts.

Write out your plan so you don't get lost as you go. Having a written plan also helps you feel more in control of the study, so anxiety is less likely to arise from feeling overwhelmed at the amount to cover.

STEP 3: GATHER YOUR TOOLS

Decide what study method works best for you. Do you prefer to highlight in the book as you study and then go back over the highlighted portions? Or do you type out notes of the important information? Or is it helpful to make flashcards that you can carry with you? Assemble the pens, index cards, highlighters, post-it notes, and any other materials you may need so you won't be distracted by getting up to find things while you study.

If you're having a hard time retaining the information or organizing your notes, experiment with different methods. For example, try color-coding by subject with colored pens, highlighters, or post-it notes. If you learn better by hearing, try recording yourself reading your notes so you can listen while in the car, working out, or simply sitting at your desk. Ask a friend to quiz you from your flashcards, or try teaching someone the material to solidify it in your mind.

STEP 4: CREATE YOUR ENVIRONMENT

It's important to avoid distractions while you study. This includes both the obvious distractions like visitors and the subtle distractions like an uncomfortable chair (or a too-comfortable couch that makes you want to fall asleep). Set up the best study environment possible: good lighting and a comfortable work area. If background music helps you focus, you may want to turn it on, but otherwise keep the room quiet. If you are using a computer to take notes, be sure you don't have any other windows open, especially applications like social media, games, or anything else that could distract you. Silence your phone and turn off notifications. Be sure to keep water close by so you stay hydrated while you study (but avoid unhealthy drinks and snacks).

Also, take into account the best time of day to study. Are you freshest first thing in the morning? Try to set aside some time then to work through the material. Is your mind clearer in the afternoon or evening? Schedule your study session then. Another method is to study at the same time of day that you will take the test, so that your brain gets used to working on the material at that time and will be ready to focus at test time.

STEP 5: STUDY!

Once you have done all the study preparation, it's time to settle into the actual studying. Sit down, take a few moments to settle your mind so you can focus, and begin to follow your study plan. Don't give in to distractions or let yourself procrastinate. This is your time to prepare so you'll be ready to fearlessly approach the test. Make the most of the time and stay focused.

Of course, you don't want to burn out. If you study too long you may find that you're not retaining the information very well. Take regular study breaks. For example, taking five minutes out of every hour to walk briskly, breathing deeply and swinging your arms, can help your mind stay fresh.

As you get to the end of each chapter or section, it's a good idea to do a quick review. Remind yourself of what you learned and work on any difficult parts. When you feel that you've mastered the material, move on to the next part. At the end of your study session, briefly skim through your notes again.

But while review is helpful, cramming last minute is NOT. If at all possible, work ahead so that you won't need to fit all your study into the last day. Cramming overloads your brain with more information than it can process and retain, and your tired mind may struggle to recall even previously learned information when it is overwhelmed with last-minute study. Also, the urgent nature of cramming and the stress placed on your brain contribute to anxiety. You'll be more likely to go to the test feeling unprepared and having trouble thinking clearly.

So don't cram, and don't stay up late before the test, even just to review your notes at a leisurely pace. Your brain needs rest more than it needs to go over the information again. In fact, plan to finish your studies by noon or early afternoon the day before the test. Give your brain the rest of the day to relax or focus on other things, and get a good night's sleep. Then you will be fresh for the test and better able to recall what you've studied.

STEP 6: TAKE A PRACTICE TEST

Many courses offer sample tests, either online or in the study materials. This is an excellent resource to check whether you have mastered the material, as well as to prepare for the test format and environment.

Check the test format ahead of time: the number of questions, the type (multiple choice, free response, etc.), and the time limit. Then create a plan for working through them. For example, if you have 30 minutes to take a 60-question test, your limit is 30 seconds per question. Spend less time on the questions you know well so that you can take more time on the difficult ones.

If you have time to take several practice tests, take the first one open book, with no time limit. Work through the questions at your own pace and make sure you fully understand them. Gradually work up to taking a test under test conditions: sit at a desk with all study materials put away and set a timer. Pace yourself to make sure you finish the test with time to spare and go back to check your answers if you have time.

After each test, check your answers. On the questions you missed, be sure you understand why you missed them. Did you misread the question (tests can use tricky wording)? Did you forget the information? Or was it something you hadn't learned? Go back and study any shaky areas that the practice tests reveal.

Taking these tests not only helps with your grade, but also aids in combating test anxiety. If you're already used to the test conditions, you're less likely to worry about it, and working through tests until you're scoring well gives you a confidence boost. Go through the practice tests until you feel comfortable, and then you can go into the test knowing that you're ready for it.

Test Tips

On test day, you should be confident, knowing that you've prepared well and are ready to answer the questions. But aside from preparation, there are several test day strategies you can employ to maximize your performance.

First, as stated before, get a good night's sleep the night before the test (and for several nights before that, if possible). Go into the test with a fresh, alert mind rather than staying up late to study.

Try not to change too much about your normal routine on the day of the test. It's important to eat a nutritious breakfast, but if you normally don't eat breakfast at all, consider eating just a protein bar. If you're a coffee drinker, go ahead and have your normal coffee. Just make sure you time it so that the caffeine doesn't wear off right in the middle of your test. Avoid sugary beverages, and drink enough water to stay hydrated but not so much that you need a restroom break 10 minutes into the test. If your test isn't first thing in the morning, consider going for a walk or doing a light workout before the test to get your blood flowing.

Allow yourself enough time to get ready, and leave for the test with plenty of time to spare so you won't have the anxiety of scrambling to arrive in time. Another reason to be early is to select a good seat. It's helpful to sit away from doors and windows, which can be distracting. Find a good seat, get out your supplies, and settle your mind before the test begins.

When the test begins, start by going over the instructions carefully, even if you already know what to expect. Make sure you avoid any careless mistakes by following the directions.

Then begin working through the questions, pacing yourself as you've practiced. If you're not sure on an answer, don't spend too much time on it, and don't let it shake your confidence. Either skip it and come back later, or eliminate as many wrong answers as possible and guess among the remaining ones. Don't dwell on these questions as you continue—put them out of your mind and focus on what lies ahead.

Be sure to read all of the answer choices, even if you're sure the first one is the right answer. Sometimes you'll find a better one if you keep reading. But don't second-guess yourself if you do immediately know the answer. Your gut instinct is usually right. Don't let test anxiety rob you of the information you know.

If you have time at the end of the test (and if the test format allows), go back and review your answers. Be cautious about changing any, since your first instinct tends to be correct, but make sure you didn't misread any of the questions or accidentally mark the wrong answer choice. Look over any you skipped and make an educated guess.

At the end, leave the test feeling confident. You've done your best, so don't waste time worrying about your performance or wishing you could change anything. Instead, celebrate the successful completion of this test. And finally, use this test to learn how to deal with anxiety even better next time.

> **Review Video: Test Anxiety**
> Visit mometrix.com/academy and enter code: 100340

Important Qualification

Not all anxiety is created equal. If your test anxiety is causing major issues in your life beyond the classroom or testing center, or if you are experiencing troubling physical symptoms related to your anxiety, it may be a sign of a serious physiological or psychological condition. If this sounds like your situation, we strongly encourage you to seek professional help.

Additional Bonus Material

Due to our efforts to try to keep this book to a manageable length, we've created a link that will give you access to all of your additional bonus material:

mometrix.com/bonus948/cast

LANGUAGE ARTS 1109
RESEARCH

LIFEPAC Test is located in the center of the booklet. Please remove before starting the unit.

Author:
Carolyn C. Goodwin, M.Ed.

Editor:
Alan Christopherson, M.S.

Media Credits:
Pages 6: © phive2015, iStock, Thinkstock; **11:** © photoquest7, iStock, Thinkstock; **16:** © Pixland, Thinkstock; **18:** © Jetta Productions, Photodisc, Thinkstock; **27:** © Maxim Kazmin, Hemera, Thinkstock; **28:** © Wavebreakmedia Ltd, iStock, Thinkstock; **37:** © Liderina, iStock, Thinkstock; **38:** © XiXinXing, iStock, Thinkstock; **46:** © sutichak, iStock, Thinkstock.

Alpha Omega
PUBLICATIONS

804 N. 2nd Ave. E.
Rock Rapids, IA 51246-1759

Research

Introduction

God gave people inquisitive minds. Their inquisitiveness compels them to find the answers to questions, to seek the truth, and to satisfy their desire to know.

Scientists and researchers conduct experiments to satisfy their inquisitiveness. Others read and collect the available information and form conclusions from their reading.

Most people have a subject they would like to know more about or a problem they would like to solve. They can learn more about the subject of their interest by reading and studying the writings of others.

In this LIFEPAC® you will learn where and how to find information on a subject that interests you. In addition, you will learn how to bring the information together into an original research paper that may be of interest to others.

Objectives

Read these objectives. The objectives tell you what you will be able to do when you have successfully completed this LIFEPAC. When you have finished this LIFEPAC, you will be able to:

1. Define the investigative process.

2. Describe the way to choose a subject for a research paper.

3. Define a thesis statement.

4. List three characteristics of a thesis statement.

5. Name major sources of information.

6. Describe the way to locate materials in the library.

7. Explain the necessary information for bibliography cards.

8. Identify primary, secondary, and tertiary sources.

9. Describe the process of note taking.

10. Describe the parts of the formal outline.

11. Explain the way to write a formal research paper.

12. Describe the proper form for citations.

Survey the LIFEPAC. Ask yourself some questions about this study and write your questions here.

_____
_____
_____
_____
_____
_____
_____
_____
_____
_____
_____
_____
_____

1. THE INVESTIGATIVE PROCESS

Research is the process of investigating or seeking facts that will lead to the truth about something. That truth is assembled from the facts a person finds during the investigation.

The writer of a research paper discovers the facts about his or her subject by reading material related to the subject under investigation, taking notes from that material, and presenting the truth of the subject in a paper.

In this section you will learn more about the investigative process. You will choose a subject for a research paper, formulate a thesis, and become acquainted with various general sources of information.

Section Objectives

Review these objectives. When you have completed this section, you should be able to:

1. Define the investigative process.
2. Describe the way to choose a subject for a research paper.
3. Define a thesis statement.
4. List three characteristics of a thesis statement.
5. Name major sources of information.

Vocabulary

Study these words to enhance your learning success in this section.

analyze   facet   pursue

cardiovascular   microcosm   ramification

evaluate

Note: *All vocabulary words in this LIFEPAC appear in* **boldface** *print the first time they are used. If you are not sure of the meaning when you are reading, study the definitions given.*

During the investigative process, a person learns to select, evaluate, and analyze the facts. A person also learns to think and to create a new and different way of looking at the subject. In this sense the research paper is original and important enough to justify the work involved.

CHOOSING A SUBJECT

Choosing a suitable subject for a research paper is important. Because of the time the writer will spend in researching the subject, the subject must be one that is interesting to the writer. The subject should also be one that merits extensive research and one that can be thoroughly developed in the number of words required.

In addition, the subject should be capable of being researched. A subject that has been written about

sparingly is a good choice for a doctoral student in college but is a poor choice for a high school student. The high school student must rely on a variety of sources that have been written by others. The subject must also be one that can be developed with facts. A personal subject that reflects the writer's opinions is not suitable for a research paper. The history of a person's life is also inappropriate for a research paper subject.

| Limit the subject.

Complete these activities.

1.1 Read the list of subjects. On the blank indicate the appropriateness of the subject for a research paper by writing *appropriate* or *not appropriate*.

a. _____ My experiences at deep-sea fishing in San Diego, California.

b. _____ Proper equipment for scuba diving.

c. _____ The history of my hometown from 1800 to 1900.

d. _____ The early life of Eleanor Roosevelt.

e. _____ Why driver education should be offered free of charge at my high school.

Complete this activity.

1.2 On the lines write the reason that each of the subjects you marked *not appropriate* in Activity 1.1 is not appropriate. Indicate the letter of each inappropriate subject.

a. _____

b. _____

c. _____

Broad subject. A writer should begin the search for a subject by examining broad areas of interest. These areas are then broken down into less general subjects. For example, a person might be interested in sports. Sports is obviously too broad a topic for a research paper. The subject contains too many specific sports to yield in-depth information. The writer would be forced to write several volumes on sports or would be able to give only a general overview of each sport.

Limited subject. Within the general subject of sports are many smaller subjects. Some of them are individual sports, such as football, basketball, and tennis. The writer begins to think about which sports are of particular interest to him. If the sport of most interest is tennis, the writer examines that subject to determine if it can be broken down into even smaller subjects. The subject *tennis* contains such limited subjects as tennis equipment, rules, clothing, techniques, and courts.

Choosing a subject, then, involves deciding on a broad area of interest, limiting its scope to a less general subject, and limiting that less general subject to a very specific subject that can be researched and written about in the number of words assigned.

Complete this activity.

1.3 Read the following list of subjects. On each line, write *broad* or *limited* to show the acceptability of the subject for a research paper.

a. _____ How to Choose a Ten-Speed Bicycle

b. _____ Nutrition

c. _____ Farming in the Middle Atlantic States

d. _____ How to Make Paper in Your Own Home

e. _____ Jogging

READING FOR BACKGROUND MATERIAL

After the writer has chosen a subject that is interesting, appropriate for research, and limited, he should begin to gather background information by reading one or two general articles on the subject. Reading a general article helps the writer determine whether the subject is too broad or too narrow and whether others have studied the subject.

An encyclopedia article provides general information on the subject. Many encyclopedias are now online at schools or local libraries. Be careful that you use reputable encyclopedias. Some encyclopedias online are not checked by editors for factual errors. Wikipedia is an example of a source that is not professionally edited.

Encyclopedias are excellent sources for general information. They help the writer see the possibilities and **ramifications** of the subject. These general information articles also help the writer become more familiar with the area in which he is working. Other general sources that provide effective background information are chapters in textbooks, histories, biographical references, and other specialized dictionaries. Most libraries have reference librarians who can help you find appropriate books and online sources.

Complete these activities.

1.4 Read an article from an online or print encyclopedia on the Bible. Answer the following questions.

a. From what language is the word *Bible* taken? _____

b. What is the meaning of the word *Bible*? _____

_____

_____

c. In what language was the New Testament originally written? _____

d. What is meant by the *canon*? _____

_____

1.5 Choose a general subject for a research paper. Limit the subject. Read a general article on the subject and name its source. On a separate sheet of paper, write a brief summary of the information you have discovered.

✓ **CHECK** _____ _____

Teacher   Date

FORMULTAING A THESIS STATEMENT

The thesis statement is a general statement that summarizes the main idea and the purpose of the research paper. It expresses in a complete sentence the problem that the writer intends to solve or the truth that the writer will attempt to verify in this paper. A thesis statement is usually an hypothesis or a theory the writer has developed from his general reading about the subject. Often a writer finds the idea for the thesis statement included in a sentence in an encyclopedia article or a textbook chapter. The thesis statement is the unsolved problem that the writer wishes to pursue or prove. The writer then attempts to prove this thesis by presenting facts and examples in his paper.

The thesis acts as a controlling agent for the entire paper. Often called a statement of purpose, the thesis states the main idea and the intention of the author directly or indirectly, guiding the writer in his research and writing.

Thesis: "A balanced diet coupled with increased exercise is the most effective method for lifetime weight control." (purpose implied)

Thesis: "The purpose of this paper is to prove that a balanced diet and exercise is the most effective method for lifetime weight control." (purpose stated)

A thesis statement should have three characteristics. It must be restricted, precise, and unified.

Complete this activity.

1.6   From the encyclopedia article about the Bible or the source you read in Activity 1.5, write three appropriate thesis statements.

a. _____

_____

_____

b. _____

_____

_____

c. _____

_____

_____

On the lines under each topic, write a thesis statement that *implies* purpose (a) and one that *states* purpose (b).

1.7   Teenage marriages

a. _____

_____

b. _____

_____

1.8   A cat's eye

a. _____

_____

b. _____

_____

1.9   A small town

a. _____

_____

b. _____

_____

Restricted. The thesis statement must be restricted. The method for restricting a thesis statement is the same as for limiting a general subject. The unrestricted thesis statement is broken into parts and the writer concentrates on the part that is most interesting or that can yield the most information. An unrestricted thesis is too general or covers too much material, just as a general subject covers too much material.

The unrestricted thesis statement, "exercise is essential at all ages," is unrestricted because it suggests too many **facets** that need to be explored. The writer should ask himself, "What type of exercise will I discuss? Why is exercise important? What are the benefits of exercise? What will happen if a person does not exercise?" After restricting the topic, the writer might decide that specific types of exercises are beneficial for certain individuals; and he might restrict the thesis statement this way: "Physical activity that exercises the heart muscle is essential for a healthy life." Thus, the thesis statement becomes restricted and capable of being developed in a paper.

Complete these activities.

1.10 Write *restricted* on the blanks next to the thesis statements that are restricted. Write *unrestricted* on the blanks next to the thesis statements that are not restricted.

a. _____ Refinishing antique furniture is a precise art.

b. _____ Art can be a profitable hobby.

c. _____ Classical music is the basis for most rock music.

d. _____ The causes of the Vietnam War were primarily economic.

e. _____ Sports exercise the mind as well as the body.

1.11 Rewrite the thesis statements from the previous activity (1.10) that were *unrestricted* to make them restricted. Indicate the letter of each rewritten sentence.

_____

_____

_____

_____

Precise. The thesis statement must be precise. It should be stated so that it has only one interpretation. A thesis statement such as "My hometown is one of the most interesting in the state" does not sufficiently indicate the content. The word *interesting* is vague because it has many meanings. The structure of the sentence also leaves the reader to wonder, "the most interesting what? the most interesting hometown?" The question cannot be answered accurately. If the hometown is what is interesting, the reader would like to know in what way it is interesting. A more precise thesis statement about the writer's hometown might be "My hometown is a **microcosm** of big city life."

Complete these activities.

1.12 Write *precise* on the blanks next to the thesis statements that are precise. Write *not precise* on the blanks next to the thesis statements that are not precise.

a. _____ Where teachers are concerned, all that glitters is not gold.

b. _____ Football is an expensive sport.

c. _____ Russian is a difficult language to learn.

d. _____ The domesticated house cat requires intelligent care if it is to reach its life expectancy.

e. _____ Fashion fads are here today, gone tomorrow.

1.13 Rewrite the thesis statements from the previous activity (1.12) that were *not precise* to make them precise. Indicate the letter of each rewritten sentence.

_____

_____

_____

_____

Unified. A thesis statement is unified when it expresses only one idea. If a writer says, "Jogging is an inexpensive activity that provides maximum exercise for the **cardiovascular** system as well as helping an individual overcome stress," the writer has said three things about jogging: (1) Jogging is inexpensive, (2) jogging is good for the cardiovascular system, and (3) jogging is effective in alleviating stress. If the writer discusses all three aspects of jogging, he will have a three-part paper which does not center on any one of the ideas. The writer should decide which of the three items about jogging he wants to stress and should concentrate on only one of them.

Complete this activity.

1.14   Write *unified* on the blanks next to the thesis statements that are unified. Write *not unified* on the blanks next to the thesis statements that are not unified.

a. _____   Private retirement systems have grown in the past twenty years because they provide extensive benefits to self-employed people.

b. _____   Private school enrollment has increased in the past five years because parents have lost confidence in the public schools and are willing to pay the additional cost to enroll their children in private schools.

c. _____   House plants can be hazardous to your health.

d. _____   Teen magazines are an inexpensive source of well-written fiction and nonfiction.

e. _____   Raising earthworms is an enjoyable and profitable hobby.

1.15   Rewrite the thesis statements in the previous activity (1.14) that were *not unified* so that they are unified. Indicate the letter of each rewritten sentence.

_____

_____

_____

_____

_____

Complete this activity.

1.16   Write a thesis statement for the subject you chose for your research paper.

_____

✔ **CHECK** _____ _____
                                                    Teacher   Date

↻ **Review the material in this section in preparation for the Self Test.** The Self Test will check your mastery of this particular section. The items missed on this Self Test will indicate specific areas where restudy is needed for mastery.

SELF TEST 1

Answer *true* **or** *false* (each answer, 1 point).

1.01 _____ Researchers attempt to find the truth about a subject.

1.02 _____ In a research paper the ideas expressed are supported by the writer's opinion.

1.03 _____ A side benefit of research is that the writer learns to evaluate and analyze information.

1.04 _____ A fact is an idea that can be verified.

1.05 _____ A good subject for a research paper is one that relies heavily on the writer's experience.

1.06 _____ A researcher might read an encyclopedia article about his subject to gain general information.

1.07 _____ The purpose of the research paper can never be stated in the thesis.

Complete these statements (each answer, 3 points).

1.08 During research, a person learns to a. _____ , b. _____ , and c. _____ the facts.

1.09 The process of seeking facts that will lead to the truth is called _____

_____ .

1.010 If many areas for exploration exist within a subject, that subject is too _____ .

1.011 Three reference books in which a person finds general information about a subject are

a. _____ , b. _____ , and c. _____ .

1.012 A general statement that summarizes the main idea and the purpose of the research paper is

the _____ .

1.013 A suitable subject for a research paper is one that is interesting to the writer, one that merits extensive research, one that can be thoroughly developed in the length required, and one that is

_____ .

Mark the following subjects *too broad*, *adequate*, **or** *limited* (each answer, 3 points).

1.014 _____ Football

1.015 _____ The Feeding Habits of the Golden Finch

1.016 _____ Farming in the Middle Atlantic States

1.017 _____ Career Opportunities in the 2020s

1.018 _____ Indian Burial Grounds in Arizona

1.019 _____ Why English Spelling Is Illogical

1.020 _____ The Benefits of Aerobic Exercise to the Cardiovascular System

1.021 _____ Ghost Towns of the Western United States

1.022 _____ Edible Underwater Plants

Write a limited subject for each of those you marked *too broad* **in numbers 1.014–1.022. Indicate the number of each rewritten subject** (each answer, 5 points).

1.023 _____

_____

1.024 _____

_____

1.025 _____

_____

1.026 _____

_____

1.027 _____

_____

1.028 _____

_____

Mark the following sentences as *not unified*, *not precise*, *unrestricted*, **or** *adequate* (each answer, 3 points).

1.029 _____ During my first week of high school, I didn't know whether I was coming or going.

1.030 _____ Solar energy is an effective means of heating new schools.

1.031 _____ Moisture creams do nothing for the skin but make it feel moister.

1.032 _____ Basketball is America's most popular sport.

1.033 _____ Running every day can be both healthful and mentally rewarding.

1.034 _____ Noncompetitive games increase honest communication among family members.

1.035 _____ Life as a teenager leaves something to be desired.

$\dfrac{92}{115}$ **SCORE** _____ ✓ **CHECK** _____ _____

Teacher   Date

2. THE LIBRARY

In Jesus's time most information was spread by word of mouth. Rarely was information recorded and preserved because writing materials were primitive. The wisest sayings of the greatest teachers in Biblical times were eventually recorded on stone or parchment and stored in temples and churches.

Through the years, as inks and paper became plentiful and more people became educated enough to write, information became extensively recorded and accumulated in libraries. The first libraries were often church-related because the churches were the seats of scholarly thought. Today, libraries are prevalent in most communities and in schools and colleges.

In this section you will learn to locate materials in the library and learn to use bibliography cards to record primary, secondary, and tertiary sources. You will have the opportunity to take notes from sources.

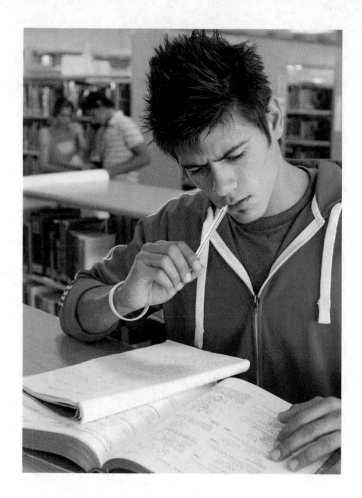

Section Objectives

Review the following objectives. When you have completed this section, you should be able to:

6. Describe the way to locate materials in the library.
7. Explain the necessary information for bibliography cards.
8. Identify primary, secondary, and tertiary sources.
9. Describe the process of note taking.

Vocabulary

Study these words to enhance your learning success in this section.

annotate	edition	plagiarism
anthology	editorial	simultaneous
bias	objective	vested interest
context	paramount	
documented	pertinent	

USING SOURCES

Libraries vary from community to community and from school to school. For this reason the researcher must familiarize himself with the library he uses to research the topic he has chosen for his paper.

If the library is totally unfamiliar to him, the researcher should spend an hour or two learning about that particular library. The librarian can be helpful, but the researcher can also learn the layout of the library on his own. Most libraries provide maps of their facilities and clear directions to the locations of books and magazines. The researcher should also learn the hours when the library is open, rules about checking out books and obtaining a library card, and any other rules that are peculiar to the library. The librarian at the checkout desk can provide that information.

The researcher should become familiar with the online resources available through the library. Most libraries have computers where you can browse their collections. These databases tell you what

books the library owns and where they are located on their shelves. You can use the database to find books based on authors, titles, or subjects. If you have questions on a how to use a library's computer catalog, ask a librarian for assistance.

The methods of cataloging books vary among libraries. Some libraries use the Dewey Decimal System while others use the Library of Congress method. The researcher needs to understand which method is used by the particular library. Noting the method is particularly important if the researcher obtains material from multiple libraries using differing methods.

When a researcher looks at the cataloging system of a library, he will notice a variety of information about a book. Much of this information is abbreviated and coded. Look at the sample information from the catalog of two libraries. The first library uses the Dewey Decimal System while the second uses the Library of Congress.

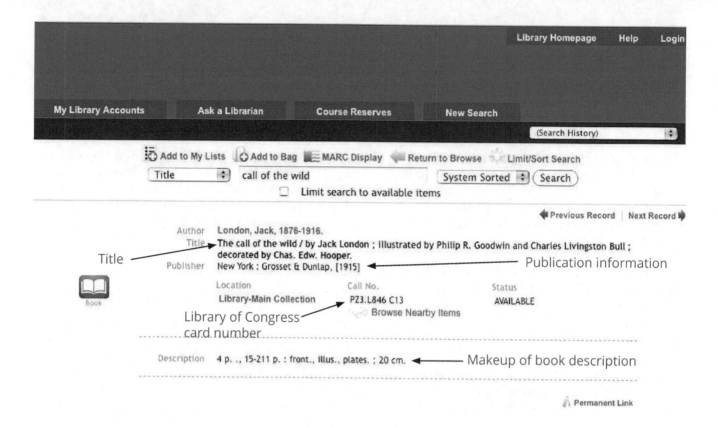

Computers have become an important part of libraries. Library patrons can locate books, movies, music, and other resources located within the library. Additionally, many libraries have computers where patrons can access the Internet. Libraries also use computers to check out books and other materials for patrons.

Rather than subscribe to hundreds of magazines, most libraries subscribe to services where people can search for articles online. EBSCO host is one search engine subscribed to by many local and community libraries. This search engine allows you to search by title, author, subject, and additional criteria. You will notice on the example that the search for hybrid cars brought 1905 matches. If you were doing this search, you would need to find ways to narrow your search. You may want to look for articles that were written in the last two years, are full text, or found in newspapers. You could also use some of the suggestions to limit your topic that are found on the bottom left-hand side of the page. For example, you could research hybrid electric cars. Whatever your research topic, you will find that the library is a great place to go for answers. If you have questions or need help, librarians are there to assist you.

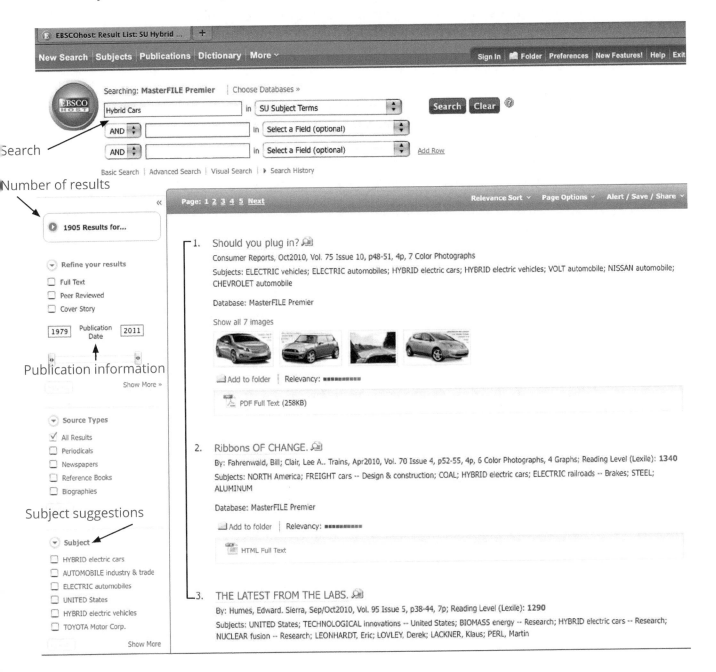

Complete this activity.

2.1   Go to the library you plan to use for the majority of your research and answer the following questions about that library.

  a. What hours is the library open? _____

  b. Does the library have a computerized system for searching for articles in magazines and newspapers?

  _____

  c. Do you need a library card to use the computers? Is there a time limit?

  _____

  d. Where are reference sources shelved?

  _____

  e. Where are magazines and periodicals located?

  _____

  f. Does your library use the Dewey Decimal System, the Library of Congress method, or some other system for cataloging books?

  _____

  g. How many books did you find in the library's holdings that pertain to your subject?

  _____

  _____

  h. How many books did you find in the computer (or the card catalog) that pertain to your subject?

  _____

  i. How does a person obtain a library card at your library?

  _____

✓ **CHECK** _____ _____
              Teacher   Date

Before a researcher begins to scan the available literature for information on the chosen topic, he must be able to differentiate between three kinds of sources, *primary*, *secondary*, and *tertiary*.

Primary. A *primary* source is the original written work on a subject, or in the case of scientific research, the original research or experiment. For example, the novel or a poem of an author is the primary source. When the researcher examines that poem or novel and comes to his own conclusions about it, the researcher is using a primary source. If a scientist conducts an experiment, that experiment is a primary source.

Secondary. A *secondary* source is a report, article, or book written about the primary source. For example, if a person examines a novel or a poem and writes an article or book about it, that article or book is a secondary source. The report a scientist writes in which he interprets the results of his experiment is also a secondary source.

Tertiary. A *tertiary* source is a third-hand account of primary material. A writer may write about the report of an experiment, or a literary critic might write concerning something someone else has said about a novel or poem. These items are both tertiary sources. Summaries of textbook chapters and encyclopedia articles are almost always tertiary sources. Researchers should generally avoid tertiary sources because truth can be lost when an idea has been interpreted by two or three people. The researcher should always keep in mind that getting as close as possible to the truth is **paramount** in any type of research. Tertiary sources are three times removed from the primary source or the truth.

Complete this activity.

2.2 Label each source as *primary*, *secondary*, or *tertiary*.

a. _____ A summary at the end of a scientific textbook

b. _____ A critical study of a poem by Robert Louis Stevenson

c. _____ The book *Little Women* by Louisa May Alcott

d. _____ An experiment a student conducts in chemistry class

e. _____ An article on the detrimental effects of eating too much sugar

f. _____ A book of interpretations of various books of the Bible

g. _____ An original oil painting

h. _____ A newspaper account of the latest press conference by the president of the United States

PREPARING A BIBLIOGRAPHY

A bibliography is the accumulation of the sources the researcher uses to support the truth of his thesis statement. The bibliographical information is recorded on 3" × 5" index cards. The researcher uses a separate card for each source. A typical bibliography card for a book will look like the one shown.

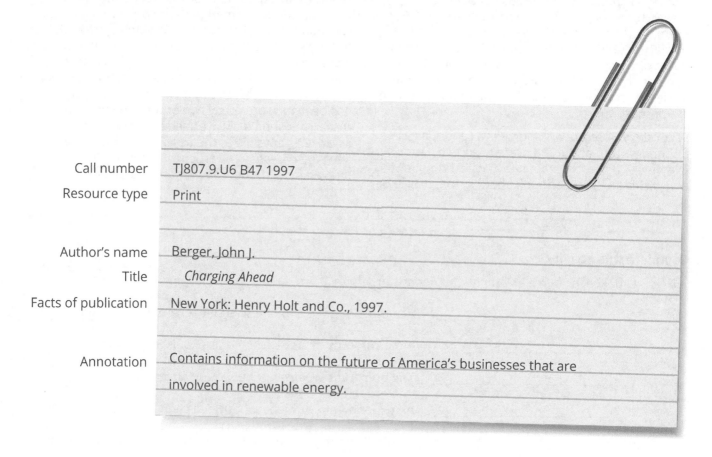

Call number	TJ807.9.U6 B47 1997
Resource type	Print
Author's name	Berger, John J.
Title	*Charging Ahead*
Facts of publication	New York: Henry Holt and Co., 1997.
Annotation	Contains information on the future of America's businesses that are involved in renewable energy.

The bibliography card contains essential information. The author's name, name of the publication, title of the article (if the entry is a magazine, newspaper, or essay), and the facts of publication are necessary for the citations and the *works cited* page of the research paper. Titles of longer works, such as books, magazines, and newspapers are always underlined or italicized. Titles of magazine articles and other shorter works are enclosed in quotation marks. The call number is essential should the researcher need to locate the publication again. Under the call number write the resource type such as print or web resource. The researcher **annotates** a source if he is reviewing many sources at one time and plans to take notes on them later. This process can save time for a researcher. When he rereads the annotation later, he remembers the information he hoped to get from the source.

Books. Books are the most common sources of information for a researcher. Various types of books, including **editions** and **anthologies**, require slightly different works cited form. The following examples show the proper form, but they do not include the library call number or annotation.

Book by a single author:
> Berger, John J.
>> *Charging Ahead*
>> New York: Henry Holt and Co., 1997. Print.

Book by two authors:
> Anderson, Curtis D., and Judy Anderson
>> *Electric and Hybrid Cars: A History*
>> Jefferson, North Carolina: McFarland and Company, 2004. Print.

Book by several authors:
> Hendrickson, Chris T. et. al.
>> *Environmental Life Cycle Assessment of Goods and Services*
>> Washington, D.C.: RFF Press, 2006. Print.

An edition other than the first edition:
> Schwaller, Anthony E.
>> *Total Automotive Technology*
>> Fourth Edition
>> Florence, Kentucky: Cengage Learning, 2004. Print.

An anthology:
> Zev, Naveh
>> *Transdisciplinary Challenges in Landscape Ecology*
>> *and Restoration Ecology - An Anthology*
>> New York: Springer, 2007. Print.

An edited work:
> Johansson, Rolph and A. Rantzer, eds.
>> *Nonlinear and Hybrid Systems in Automotive Control*
>> New York: Springer-Verlag New York, LLC, 2007. Print.

Complete these activities.

2.3   Write *C* on the line if the bibliographical entry is correct and *I* if it is incorrect.

a. _____   Porter, J.R.
>> *Jesus Christ: The Jesus of History, the Christ of Faith*
>> Oxford University Press, 2007.

b. _____   Buechner, Frederick
>> *The Faces of Jesus: A Life Story*
>> Orleans, Massachusetts: Paraclete Press, 2006. Print.

c. _____   Mortenson, Greg and Relin, David Oliver.
>> *Three Cups of Tea*
>> NY: Penguin Group, 2007. Print.

d. _____   F. Scott Fitzgerald
>> *The Great Gatsby*
>> Simon and Schuster, 2004. Print.

2.4   Rewrite the bibliographical entries in Activity 2.3 that were incorrect so they are correct.

a. _____

_____

_____

b. _____

_____

_____

c. _____

_____

_____

2.5   Find two books in the library that pertain to the subject of your research paper. Make a proper bibliographical index card for each of the books. Ask another student to check your cards for correct form. Remember to list the call number and write an annotation.

✓ **CHECK** _____   _____
                                                     Teacher   Date

Magazine articles are excellent sources of information for research papers. They often provide the most current thought and research on a subject. Magazines that are filed or bound in volumes are generally cataloged by call numbers. Most libraries subscribe to services such as EBSCO host. These services allow patrons to find articles that are in magazines or newspapers that the library may not have on the shelves. You will find an example of an EBSCO host page below. Even if your library does not subscribe to *Popular Science*, you are able to read the entire article online. EBSCO host has special search engines designed for students in grades 9-12. These search engines are geared to the articles students in high school are likely to use.

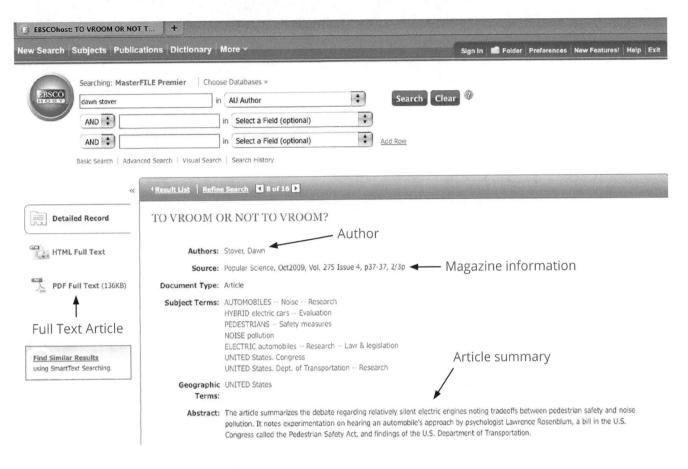

Magazine article with one author:

> Zakaria, Fareed
>> "Imagine: 500 Mile Per Gallon"
>> *Newsweek*
>> March 7, 2005
>> p. 27. Print.

The entry for magazines is much the same as the entry for books. Notice that the title of the article, enclosed in quotation marks, is written under the author's name. The date of publication of the article and the pages on which the article is found are also included. Indicate if you found the article in a print magazine or on the web.

Magazine article with more than one author:

> Hamilton, Anita, et.al.
>> "Why Hybrids are Hot"
>> *Time*
>> April 29, 2002
>> p. 52-53. Print.

Magazine article with no author:

> "The Sound of Silence"
>> *Economist*
>> May 9, 2009
>> p. 85. Web.

Complete these activities.

2.6   Write *C* on the line if the bibliographical entry is correct and *I* if it is incorrect.

a. _____   Vander Werp, David.
                        "A Hybrid That Has No Batteries"
                        Car and Driver
                        February 2009
                        p. 24. Print.

b. _____   David Owen
                        "Economy vs. Environment"
                        New Yorker
                        March 30, 2009
                        p. 21-22. Web.

c. _____   Margonelli, Lisa
                        Atlantic Monthly
                        "Down and Dirty"
                        May 2009
                        p. 17-18. Print.

d. _____   Webster, Larry
                        "Hybrid Tax Credits"
                        Popular Mechanics
                        October 2009
                        p. 37. Web.

2.7   Give the letter of the bibliographical entries in Activity 2.6 that were incorrect and rewrite the incorrect line or lines so that they are correct.

_____

_____

_____

Complete this activity.

2.8   In the library, look in EBSCO host or a similar search engine and find one magazine article that pertains to your subject. Write a bibliography card for that magazine article.

✓ **CHECK** _____   _____
                        Teacher   Date

Pamphlets. The library generally has a file of pamphlets that researchers may use in the library. Often the pamphlets provide recent information on the subject under investigation. Pamphlets by an author or authors are recorded in the same way books with an author or several authors are recorded. The following examples illustrate entries for pamphlets.

Pamphlet with an author:

Ekberg, Keith
"The Names of God in the Old Testament"
Greensville, South Carolina: The Bible Speaks Ministries
2007. Print.

Pamphlet without an author:

Used Truck Association
"What Is a Low Mileage Truck?"
Stockbridge, Georgia
2004. Print.

Complete this activity.

2.9 In the library, find a pamphlet that pertains to the subject of your research paper. Write a bibliography card for that pamphlet. If your library does not have a pamphlet about your subject, find one on a subject that interests you and write a bibliography card for it. Ask another student to review your card.

✓ **CHECK** _____ _____
                             Teacher   Date

Newspapers. Libraries often subscribe to local, regional, and national newspapers. These newspapers are generally kept no longer than a half a year to a year. Fortunately, many of the articles found in back issues of newspapers can be found online through a search engine like EBSCO host. You can use the same search engine to find newspaper and magazine articles. Researchers should avoid using editorials as resources and editorialized columns because they are opinion-based and often lack facts. The following examples illustrate newspaper entries.

Newspaper article with author:

Terlap, Sharon

"GM Hopes Volt Juice Its Future"

Wall Street Journal

September 12, 2009

Sec. B p. 2; 5. Web.

Newspaper article without author:

"Hybrid Fuels Efficiency"

Mornington Peninsula Leader

September 22, 2009

Sec. 1, p. 5. Print.

Complete this activity.

2.10 Write correct bibliography entries for newspaper articles from the information provided.

a. A newspaper writer for the *San Francisco Chronicle* named David R. Baker wrote an article called "$529 Million Loan for Plug-In Hybrids." The article can be found in section A, page 16 in the September 23, 2009 edition which was found on the web.

_____

_____

_____

_____

_____

b. Paul Grover wrote an article called "Huge Frankfurt Goes Hybrid." It was published on September 18, 2009 in the first section on the third page of the *Melbourne Herald Sun* and found in print.

_____

_____

_____

_____

c. The *Wall Street Journal* published an article entitled "Will China Tighten 'Rare Earth' Grip?" The article was written by Chuin Yap in Section C on page 12 in print.

_____

_____

_____

_____

_____

Essays. Often one essay in a collection provides valuable information for the researcher.

> Hanson, Ron
> > "Faith and Fiction"
> > > *In Shouts and Whispers*. Jennifer L. Holberg, Ed.
> > > Grand Rapids: Eerdmans, 2006. Print.

Complete these activities.

2.11   In the library find an essay that pertains to your subject. Write a bibliography card in correct form for that essay.

✓ **CHECK** _____ _____
                                    Teacher   Date

2.12   Rewrite the following references in correct bibliographical form.

a. A book by Arthur R. Simon titled *How Much is Enough?* The book was published by Baker Books in Grand Rapids, Michigan in 2003.

_____

_____

_____

b. A newspaper article entitled "People Already Care for the Needy—Without a Government Mandate" with an unknown author. The article was found in *USA Today* in section A on page 10 on July 31, 2009 in a print form.

_____

_____

_____

_____

_____

c. An article entitled "Desert Deaths" by Jeremy Weber in *Christianity Today*. It was found in the August 2009 issue on pages 8-9 in the web edition.

_____

_____

_____

_____

d. Jeanette Catsoulis wrote an article for the *New York Times* entitled "A Child's-Eye View of a Village That Subsists on Trash." It was published on September 9, 2009 and was found in the first section on page 9 in the print edition.

_____

_____

_____

_____

_____

e. The book *Two Billion Cars: Driving Toward Sustainability* written by Daniel Sperling and Deborah Gordon. The book was published by Oxford University Press in New York in 2009 and found in print form.

_____

_____

_____

_____

Complete this activity.

2.13   Find at least five sources for your research paper. Make a bibliography card for each. Include an annotation for each card.

✓ **CHECK** _____   _____
                    Teacher   Date

TAKING NOTES

Preparing the bibliography and taking notes can be a **simultaneous** process. The researcher finds a book or an article that contains pertinent information. He records the bibliographical information on a card and proceeds to take notes on that source before beginning to record information from another source.

The annotation on a bibliography card is different from actual note taking. An annotation is a short summary reminder of the contents of a source. Research notes are extensive information taken from the sources. The information is written on other index cards.

Notes are recorded most satisfactorily on cards that measure 4" × 6" or 5" × 8" because these larger cards provide more space for writing.

All note cards contain the author's name in the upper left-hand corner. The author's last name is usually sufficient unless the researcher is using

sources by different authors with the same last name. In that case, the researcher must also list the author's first name to avoid confusion later. If the same author has written more than one book or article that will be used in the research, the researcher should indicate the title of the work from which he is taking the notes. In addition, the page from which the notes are being taken should be listed next to the author's name. At the top of the card, the researcher should write a general topic heading for that note. A general topic heading is the subject for that particular note card. It is a general heading that can be changed later. However, it gives the researcher, as he reviews his cards, a general idea of topic areas he has covered. Only one idea should be expressed on each note card. This example shows how the card should look.

Reading Readiness

Weber, p. 7

One way schools determine reading readiness

is with an I.Q. test. If the child's "mental age"

is 6½, the school believes he's ready to read.

A researcher might take four types of notes: a summary note, a direct quotation, a paraphrase note, or a critical note. A *summary note* expresses the general idea of several paragraphs or pages from a source. The researcher reads several pages, closes the source, and summarizes the ideas in his own words. The summary may also be recorded in outline form.

The second type of note is a *direct quotation*. The researcher uses this type of note sparingly because in the written paper no more than 10 percent of the total number of words may be direct quotations. In addition, the researcher may be accused of **plagiarism** if he uses too many direct quotations without

references, as though the ideas were his own. The researcher should indicate on the note card when a statement is a direct quotation by enclosing the direct quotation in quotation marks. He should also be careful not to quote out of **context**. If the meaning is in doubt from the quotation alone, the researcher should quote enough so that the context is not lost.

The third type of note is a *paraphrase note*. This note is a combination of a direct quotation and the researcher's own words. Any part of this note that is a direct quotation should be enclosed by quotation marks.

The fourth type of note is the *critical note*. The researcher may read a portion of an article that is contrary to the majority of information he has learned thus far. In that case, he might note, "This article disagrees with the five other sources I have read to date." (On his note card, he would not enclose his own remarks in quotation marks.)

Similarly, the researcher might read from a source that is clearly **biased** or poorly **documented**. The researcher would note that fact on the note card. The fact that information has been published by a known publishing firm does not necessarily mean that the information is true.

Complete this activity.

2.14   Label the following notes *summary, direct quotation, paraphrase,* or *critical*.

a. _____ Author says that the discovery of zero is a great cultural accomplishment.

b. _____ 1. Policy
      A. Philosophy
      B. Law
         1. Used to govern
         2. Ethically formulated

c. _____ Dwight McDonald remarked, "In an age that was enthusiastic about social issues, Agee's whole style was individualistic and anti-scientific."

d. _____ The author's experience in Alabama strengthened his commitment: a vision "too intense to be expressed in conventional forms."

e. _____ The author's intensity in de-emphasizing the role of organized crime in the state is distressing particularly because three other authors believe organized crime is the reason the state is failing to prosper.

f. _____ The main idea of the chapter was that, to maintain some measure of self respect, a person must not let others dictate to him what his actions should be.

Researchers must be aware that a book or an article is not necessarily the truth simply because it has been published. An author may have a **vested interest** in the subject or in the publication of the book or article. A member of the tourist bureau in Hawaii who writes a book to encourage tourism in that state may not be **objective** in his presentation. The researcher who is aware of a possible lack of objectivity on the author's part can read the source carefully for an obvious slant or bias. He should also be aware of the documentation and the extent of research the author presents. A survey that uses as its sample ten school children may not be a wide enough survey for an adequate conclusion. The researcher must read carefully to learn the truth.

Complete this activity.

2.15   Record notes from your bibliographical sources on 4" × 6" or 5" × 8" note cards.

CHECK _____ _____
                 Teacher   Date

Review the material in this section in preparation for the Self Test. The Self Test will check your mastery of this particular section as well as your knowledge of the previous section.

SELF TEST 2

Complete these statements (each answer, 3 points).

2.01   Five sources that a person might use in researching a subject for a research paper are

a. _____ , b. _____ , c. _____ ,

d. _____ , and e. _____ .

2.02   A(n) _____ source is an original work written about a subject.

2.03   The three methods for cataloging books are a. _____ ,

b. _____ , and c. _____ .

2.04   An original written work or a scientist's experiment is called a(n) _____ .

2.05   A report of a magazine article about an experiment is a(n) _____ .

2.06   A critical article about a book is a(n) _____ .

2.07   The note at the bottom of a bibliography card is the _____ .

2.08   The note that expresses a general idea about a source is a(n) _____ note.

2.09   A writer who quotes directly from a source as if the ideas were his own might be accused of

_____ .

Answer *true* **or** *false* (each answer, 1 point).

2.010   _____   A note card contains the name of the author, the title of the publication, and the publication information.

2.011   _____   Direct quotations should constitute no more than 10 percent of the total words of the research paper.

2.012   _____   Magazine article titles are always underlined.

2.013   _____   Researchers must use more than one library to gain enough material for a research paper.

2.014   _____   A library's computerized catalog allows you to search only by author's last name.

2.015   _____   A tertiary source is the most desirable source for a researcher to use.

2.016   _____   An encyclopedia article is usually a secondary source.

2.017   _____   A student researcher should consult at least five varied sources for an 800- to 1,000-word research paper.

2.018   _____   When a book has an editor instead of an author, the researcher records the title and publication information only.

2.019   _____   If a book or magazine article has been published by a known publishing company, the information is probably true.

Write *correct* **or** *incorrect* **for each of the bibliographical entries** (each answer, 3 points).

2.020 _____ Li, Yading

> *Christian History and Biography*
> "Everything for the Lord"
> Spring 2008
> p. 13. Print.

2.021 _____ Isaac, Phiri and Jonathan Fitzgerald

> "Building Peace Beyond Understanding"
> *Christianity Today*
> January 2009
> p. 56-61. Web.

2.022 _____ "Medical Missionaries"

> Perla, Trevizo
> *Chattanooga Time/Free Press*
> Sept. 26, 2009. Print.

2.023 _____ Membery, York

> "It Happened to Me …"
> *Daily Mail*
> September 12, 2009
> Sec. 1, p15. Print.

2.024 _____ Meyers, Margaret

> Minneapolis: Milkweed Editions
> 1995
> *Swimming in the Congo* Web.

LANGUAGE ARTS 1109

LIFEPAC TEST

Name _____

Date _____

Score _____

58
72

LANGUAGE ARTS 1109: LIFEPAC TEST

Answer *true* **or** *false* (each answer, 1 point).

1. _____ A bibliography card contains the library call number.

2. _____ The writer's purpose or intention for the research paper can be included in the thesis statement.

3. _____ In a citation, the author's last name is written first.

4. _____ All libraries use the Dewey Decimal System.

5. _____ A fact is a statement that can be verified.

6. _____ Citations appear in the text of a research paper.

7. _____ Student writers usually provide too many details in their research papers.

8. _____ Documentation is the process of giving credit for ideas that are not the writer's own ideas.

9. _____ The introduction to the research paper should always be written first.

10. _____ If a magazine article has no author, the writer of the research paper writes "no author" on the bibliography card.

Write the letter of the correct answer on the line (each answer, 2 points).

11. Each note card that the researcher prepares contains _____ .

 a. one idea

 b. the title of the source

 c. the library call number

 d. one page of summary from the source

12. The researcher reads a page from a book. He closes the book and writes a note on a note card.

 He has written a _____ note.

 a. tertiary   b. paraphrase   c. summary   d. direct quotation

13. You can look up books by all of the following ways except _____ .

 a. subject   b. author   c. number of pages   d. title

14. Roman numerals in an outline signify _____ .

 a. details

 b. main ideas

 c. subdivisions

 d. secondary headings

15.   At the top of each note card, the researcher should write _____ .

    a. the note

    b. the title of the book or article

    c.   the library call number

    d. a general heading

Complete these statements (each answer, 3 points).

16.   The four types of notes a researcher might write are a. _____ , b. _____ ,

         c. _____ , and d. _____ .

17.   A first-hand source such as an experiment is called a(n) _____ source.

18.   The written guide the researcher uses in writing the research paper is the _____ .

19.   Four kinds of information a writer must cite are a. _____ , b. _____ ,

         c. _____ , and d. _____ .

Match these items (each answer, 2 points).

20.   _____ correct citation

21.   _____ conclusion

22.   _____ correct *works cited* page entry

23.   _____ broad subject

24.   _____ limited subject

25.   _____ annotation

26.   _____ Dewey Decimal System

27.   _____ encyclopedia article

28.   _____ order for a research paper

29.   _____ sentence or topic

30.   _____ transition

a. note at the bottom of bibliography card

b. (Jones 73).

c. bridge between sentences or paragraphs

d. Jones, Agnes. *The Beauty of God.* New York: Hanson Brothers, Inc., 1973. Print.

e. outline

f. World War II

g. summary at the end of a research paper

h. library cataloging method

i. Why English Spelling Is Illogical

j. general information source

k. time

l. date

Write the letter of the correct answer on each line (each answer, 2 points).

2.025 In the upper left-hand corner of the note card, the researcher puts _____ .

a. the call number

b. the page number

c. the author's name

d. nothing

2.026 A statement that controls the ideas expressed in the research paper is a(n) _____ .

a. thesis statement

b. purpose statement

c. tertiary note

d. annotation

2.027 At the top of each note card, the researcher writes _____ .

a. author's name

b. nothing

c. general heading

d. the page number

2.028 A restricted thesis statement should _____ .

a. contain only one idea

b. compare two items

c. be exact

d. show the writer's motivation

2.029 If the same author has written more than one article or book being used by the researcher, the

researcher should _____ .

a. discard one book or article

b. list the author's full name on the note card

c. list the book or article title on the note card

d. make out only one bibliography card

2.030 Each note card expresses _____ idea(s).

a. as many as the researcher decides to record

b. only one

c. not more than two

d. one page's

2.031 The note that may be expressed in an outline is _____ .

a. direct quotation   b. paraphrase   c. summary   d. critical

2.032 The reference that best allows people to find magazine articles listed by subject, title, author, and

additional criteria is _____ .

a. an encyclopedia

b. a newspaper

c. a computerized catalog

d. EBSCO host

69
—
86

SCORE _____

✓ **CHECK** _____ _____
                        Teacher   Date

3. THE COMPOSITION

The composition or research paper is the written product of the work the researcher has done in his attempt to solve the problem or to discover the truth expressed in the thesis statement. That truth or problem is substantiated or solved in a formal paper that contains an outline, an introduction, a precisely written body, a conclusion, citations, and works cited.

In this section you will write a formal research paper, beginning with a thesis statement that is restricted, precise, and unified. Next you will prepare a formal outline and follow it in the writing of your paper. To complete your paper, you will prepare citations in the proper form, write a title page, and properly list works cited.

Section Objectives

Review these objectives. When you have completed this section, you should be able to:

10. Describe the parts of the formal outline.

11. Explain the way to write a formal research paper.

12. Describe the proper form for citations.

Vocabulary

Study these words to enhance your learning success in this section.

chronology	consecutively	implication
climactic	contention	statistics
coherent	dialogue	substantiate

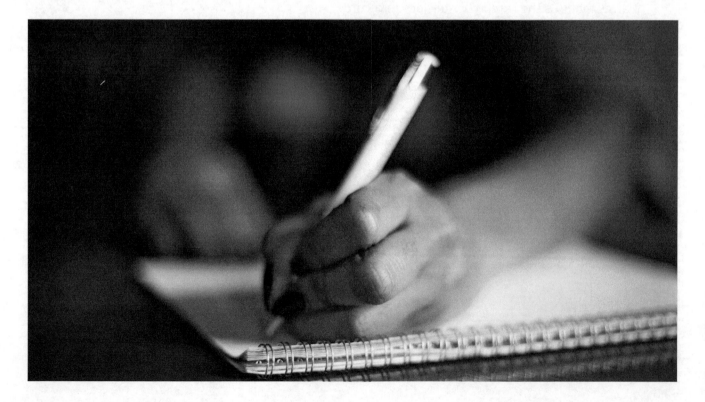

STATING THE THESIS

A review of the original thesis statement indicates whether it remains appropriate to the information the researcher has gathered on note cards. The researcher may find that the thesis statement needs refining or limiting further before he can begin to write the research paper. The researcher, therefore, evaluates the thesis statement in relationship to the notes by rereading the thesis statement for all its implications and by rereading each note card to determine if the note actually applies to the thesis statement. He then either discards those notes that are not applicable or refines the thesis statement so that it pertains directly to the notes.

For example, the researcher's thesis statement might be "Edible plants can be a decorative addition to any home." In his review of his notes, he finds that he has taken several notes on house plants that are not edible. He decides to discard the notes that do not pertain to his thesis statement because he wants to retain the original statement.

Another researcher finds that the original thesis statement needs modification. His thesis is "Mathematics anxiety in women occurs because they are not analytical thinkers." Since the available information does not support that contention, he changes the thesis statement to conform to the information he has gathered. The new thesis statement is "Mathematics anxiety in women occurs because they are discouraged by their teachers from taking advanced mathematics courses." This change in thesis statement is drastic, but it does conform to the information the researcher has gathered.

Less drastic changes in the thesis statement are usually necessary. Perhaps the previously mentioned researcher finds that women experience mathematics anxiety because their teachers often do not encourage their analytical thinking. The researcher would then make only minor changes in the original thesis statement. Perhaps it would read "Women experience mathematics anxiety because their teachers discourage their efforts at analytical thinking."

Complete these activities.

3.1   The following sentences and the accompanying notes do not correspond. Write a thesis statement revision that does correspond to the notes, or list by number the notes you would discard.

a. Thesis: Ability grouping in schools is detrimental to slower students.

   Notes: 1. Bright students gain from being in class with both average and slow students.
             2. Slower students are deprived of the intellectual stimulation of more advanced students.
             3. Slow students develop poor self-images.
             4. Teachers spend less time with slow students when they know these students are slow.
             5. The average student is the forgotten student in the school with ability grouping.

   _____

   _____

   _____

b. Thesis: IQ test scores do not necessarily define a person's intelligence.

   Notes: 1. IQ tests do not measure a person's ability to learn a new skill.
             2. Interest inventories chart a person's preference for certain activities.
             3. IQ tests have been shown to have a cultural bias.
             4. IQ tests actually measure a person's knowledge.
             5. IQ tests measure a person's ability to reason and think logically.

   _____

   _____

   _____

c. Thesis: During the Civil War, my hometown was a strategic link in the Underground Railroad.

   Notes: 1. Runaway slaves were hidden by local residents.
             2. My great-grandfather transported more than three hundred slaves across the state line in his hay wagon.
             3. Today, the children of many former slaves live in my hometown.
             4. My hometown was first settled by the English in 1700.

   _____

   _____

   _____

3.2   Evaluate your own thesis statement and the notes you have taken. Make changes in the thesis statement that are necessary. Discard any notes that do not apply. Write the final thesis statement here.

✓ **CHECK** _____   _____
                   Teacher   Date

OUTLINING THE PAPER

Because the research paper is usually long and complex, it always requires a careful outline. A detailed outline, in fact, is a critical state in the preparation of the paper. The researcher should never begin to write the paper until the outline has been thoroughly and completely developed.

Framing of the outline begins with the researcher's note card headings. As the researcher took notes, he wrote a general heading at the top of each note card. These headings now become the main divisions in the outline. Another careful review of the notes indicate which notes **substantiate** the main divisions and are therefore further subdivisions of the main division. Other notes may be further divisions of the subdivision notes. The researcher may discover as he reviews his notes that some headings need to be changed before the outline can be completed. After the necessary changes he can begin to develop the outline.

Complete this activity.

3.3   Re-evaluate your note cards. Make necessary changes in the general headings so that you have at least three general areas which relate to the thesis statement. List those general areas on these lines.

I.   _____

II.   _____

III. _____

 CHECK _____ _____

Teacher   Date

Topic outline. Two types of outlines are a topic outline and a sentence outline. A topic outline is developed with headings consisting of single words or phrases that identify the topic to be discussed under each heading. The following example illustrates two sections of a topic outline.

Thesis statement: The tale of "Cinderella" has evolved from a charming bedtime story to a profitable money-maker.

I. "Cinderella" as a fairy tale
    A. Appeal to Children
        1. Fantasy
        2. Magic
        3. Happy ending
    B. Structure of Story
        1. Easily told
        2. Easily remembered
        3. Lesson taught

(continued on next page)

    II. "Cinderella" as a profitable money-maker
      A. Media
        1. Films
        2. Radio
        3. Advertisements
        4. Recordings
        5. Books
      B. Merchandise
        1. Disneyland
        2. Saleables
          a. Watches
          b. Toys
          c. Clothing
          d. Furniture

Sentence Outline. In a sentence outline each entry is a complete sentence. Each sentence identifies the topic and what is said about the topic. Because it tells what is to be said about the topic, the sentence outline helps the writer maintain control of the subject. This example illustrates two sections of a sentence outline.

Thesis statement: The tale of "Cinderella" has evolved from a charming bedtime story to a profitable money-maker.

I. "Cinderella" was originally a charming bedtime story.
    A. "Cinderella" appealed to children.
      1. It was a fantasy.
      2. It contained magic.
      3. It had a happy ending.
    B. "Cinderella" had simple story structure.
      1. Its plot was simple.
      2 It was easily remembered.
      3. It contained an easily discerned lesson.
II. "Cinderella" is now a profitable business.
    A. The media have benefited.
      1. Films tell the story of "Cinderella."
      2. Television shows "Cinderella" in cartoon form.
      3. Cinderella advertises child-oriented products.
      4. The story of "Cinderella" is a best-selling recording.
      5. The film version of "Cinderella" is now in book form.
    B. The merchants have benefited.
      1. Disneyland features a Cinderella ride.
      2. Cinderella items are for sale.
        a. Cinderella watches are top sellers.
        b. Cinderella toys are available in most toy stores.
        c. Cinderella's picture is emblazoned on clothing.
        d. Cinderella furniture is sold for children's rooms.

The person who has had little experience in writing a research paper may feel more comfortable in using the sentence outline. It requires more time to prepare because the writer must determine exactly what is to be said about each division and subdivision. The actual writing of the research paper, however, will require less time because of the controlling features of the sentence outline.

Both sentence outlines and topic outlines observe the same rules for dividing and subdividing areas of information. Roman numerals signify a main heading or section in the research paper. Capital letters signify a division in the Roman numeral topic.

If the writer divides the Roman numeral topic into an *A* subtopic, he must also have a *B* subtopic. The reason for this rule is that in order for the writer to divide an idea or topic, he must divide it into at least two parts. A person cannot divide something into one part.

The next divisions are for further subdividing into details. Arabic numerals (1, 2, 3, 4) signify details. The writer, again, must subdivide into at least two parts. Lowercase letters such as *a, b, c* signify minor details necessary for a full explanation of some topics. They must also be divided into at least two details if they are listed at all.

Complete this activity.

3.4   Organize the following material into appropriate divisions and subdivisions under the two Roman numeral headings. Write the outline in the space provided.

My Early School Days

1.   Going to assembly

2.   Learning to read

3.   Nursery school days

4.   Things I remember best in kindergarten

5.   "Graduation from kindergarten"

6.   First grade mysteries

7.   New surroundings, new teacher, new rules, schoolwork in elementary school

8.   Getting used to the routine in elementary school

9.   The cafeteria

10.   The school bus

11.   Opening days at kindergarten

12.   Early acquaintances in elementary school

13.   Friends and foes

14.   The playground

I.   Introduction to School

II.   Elementary School

Complete this activity.

3.5   Write a sentence outline and a topic outline from the information provided.

Thesis statement: Behavior modification is an effective means to control weight.

1. List kind and amount of food eaten.
2. List place and time food is eaten.
3. Keep a food diary.
4. Keep an exercise diary.
5. List any eating cues.
6. Advertisements for food may cue people to eat.
7. List time and amount of exercise.
8. Exercise must be in addition to daily activities.
9. Strenuous exercises such as jogging, jumping rope, and walking are essential.
10. Plan ahead for anticipated large or high-calorie meals.
11. All eating should be done where no other activity takes place.
12. Before beginning an exercise program, keep track of present exercise schedule.

Topic Outline

Thesis statement:

    I.
        A.
            1.
            2.
            3.
            4.
        B.
            1.
            2.
            3.
            4.
            5.
                a.
                b.
    II.
        A.
        B.
            1.
            2.
            3.
                a.
                b.
                c.

Sentence Outline

Thesis statement:

  I.

     A.

        1.

        2.

        3.

        4.

     B.

        1.

        2.

        3.

        4.

        5.

           a.

           b.

  II.

     A.

     B.

        1.

        2.

        3.

           a.

           b.

           c.

The mechanics of outlining have a distinct purpose. Each division and subdivision in the outline relates to the one it is developing and ultimately to the thesis statement. An effective check of the outline is to determine if every entry refers to the one it is developing. The capital letter entries should refer to the Roman-numeral entry they are developing, the Arabic numerals should relate to the capital letters, and so on.

Order of outline. The order of the outline parts should show a logical progression. If any parts are out of order, the disorder will be more obvious in the research paper. The writer should have a reason for the particular order that he uses. Perhaps the least important idea will come first. Perhaps the order is already determined by time, **chronology**, or sequence.

Complete this activity.

3.6   Write *time*, *chronological*, or *sequential* to indicate the order of each outline.

I. Saturdays
    A. Sleep until 10:00 A.M.
    B. Eat Breakfast
    C. Household Tasks
        1. Clean my room
        2. Mow the lawn
        3. Trim the hedge
    D. Eat Lunch
    E. Hang around with the Guys
    F. Eat Supper
    G. Listen to the Radio
    H. Go to Bed

a. _____

I. Planting Flowers
    A. Prepare the Soil
        1. Plow it
        2. Mix in topsoil
    B. Dig Furrows
    C. Place Seeds in One at a Time
    D. Cover Seeds
    E. Water

b. _____

II. Morning
    A. 6:00 A.M.
        1. Alarm goes off
        2. Put on jogging suit
    B. 6:15 A.M.
        1. Leave house to jog
        2. Meet jogging companion
    C. 7:00 A.M.
        1. Return from jogging
        2. Begin shower
    D. 7:30 A.M.
        1. Eat breakfast
        2. Read paper

c. _____

An outline is preceded by the thesis statement, which should be written on a separate line above the outline and should be labeled.

The outline, then, should contain a thesis statement and all items the writer intends to develop in the paper. The outline is the guide or map that helps the writer control the thought and flow of the paper. It should be referred to constantly during the writing of the paper.

Complete this activity.

3.7   Write the outline for your research paper.

✓ **CHECK** _____   _____
                              Teacher   Date

WRITING THE RESEARCH PAPER

With the outline satisfactorily completed, the writer can compose the research paper with relative ease. The outline, serving as a guide, need only be developed into sentences and paragraphs. Direct quotations are added where they are appropriate and in cases where the author of the source had expressed a thought so precisely that it must be used directly.

Paragraph development. The writer is wise to begin by writing the first paragraph of the body of the research paper instead of the introduction. The writer begins with his first main heading, which he develops into a topic sentence. The topic sentence is to the paragraph as the thesis statement is to the research paper. The topic sentence makes a

statement about the contents of the paragraph. It, too, should be restricted, precise, and unified.

The second sentence in the paragraph is a sentence of explanation or clarification about the topic of the paragraph. The remaining sentences express further detail about the subject of the paragraph. They may contain examples, quotations, comparisons, or statistics that further explain the idea of the paragraph. The sentences within the paragraph should follow each other in a logical progression of thought. A logical progression of ideas makes understanding easy for the reader; therefore, communication is more likely to be successful.

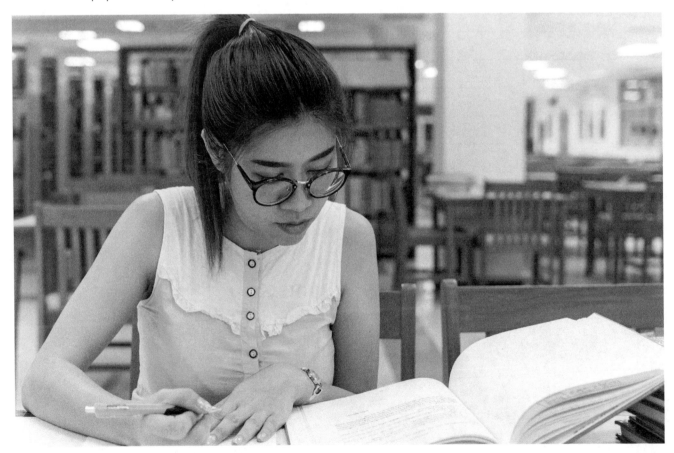

Complete these activities.

3.8   The sentences in the following paragraph are out of order. In the space provided, rewrite the paragraph so that the sentences are in logical order with topic sentence, sentences of explanation, and
detail.

Slang

Jargon, applied especially to the vocabulary of a business or profession, and *cant*, an older term
than *slang*, have come into relatively the same usage over the years. The word *slang* is derived
either from the past tense of *sling* or from *slanguage*. Mario Pei, in his book, *The Story of Language*,
says that the term slang was first used in England in the middle eighteenth century. The *s* in *slanguage* is said to come from expressions such as *thieves' language*. English literature slang, however,
goes back to the sixteenth century.

_____

_____

_____

_____

_____

_____

_____

_____

_____

_____

_____

_____

_____

_____

_____

_____

3.9   Write the first paragraph of your research paper.

✓ **CHECK** _____ _____
                    Teacher   Date

Notes. An important consideration in writing the research paper is the natural inclusion of notes and quotations. Direct quotations are often the most troublesome to include naturally because they are another person's way of saying something. The writer's own style probably varies from that of the person he is quoting. Note how unnatural this paragraph sounds when the author merely strings together the notes he has taken.

Crafting violins is a pain-staking process. "The technological method of making violins hasn't changed much in 300 years" (Waters 7). All aspects of making a violin need to be carefully crafted. "The arching of the wood on the top of the violin is one of the most important aspects of its design … the curves should extend all the way to the edge of the top to carry the vibrating sounds through the entire instrument" (Waters 7). Violin making is a challenging process. "Violin makers can produce perhaps seven top-quality instruments a year" ("Con Brio" 40).

The writer should try to weave material and quotations into the paragraphs of the research paper as the writer did in this example.

Crafting violins is a pain-staking process. The hand-crafting technique has changed little in over 300 years (Waters 7). Each section of the violin must be precisely made. Even the curves at the top of the instrument must be carefully made so that they carry the sound throughout the violin (Waters 7). Because violins must be properly made, a good maker can only produce "seven top-quality instruments a year" ("Con Brio" 40).

Complete this activity.

3.10 Rewrite the following paragraph so that the resource material flows with the remainder of the paragraph.

A person considering the cost of school athletics must first consider salaries of coaches, custodians, trainers, and band directors. James Johnson said, "Equipment is another major cost" (7). Equipment includes uniforms for athletes, marching band, pom-pom line, cheerleaders, and other groups whose function is tied to the athletics program. Equipment includes balls, bats, nets, clubs, laundry and cleaning costs, first-aid supplies, and medical supplies (Smith 39). Johnson also discusses utility costs. "Some are directly related to the sports program such as lighting and air conditioning" (23). Water used by the team for showers should be included.

_____

_____

_____

_____

_____

_____

_____

_____

_____

_____

_____

_____

_____

_____

_____

_____

_____

Direct quotations are the exact words of an author and are enclosed in quotation marks. Indirect quotations are not the exact words of the author and are not enclosed in quotation marks. An indirect quotation is often preceded by *that* or an implied *that*. These examples illustrate the difference.

Direct Quotation:

He said, "I have found considerable evidence to support my thesis statement."

Indirect Quotation:

He said that he had found considerable evidence to support his thesis statement.

He said he's found considerable evidence to support his thesis statement.

Citations. Both direct and indirect quotations need to be cited within the text. The writer should also cite information for which he is indebted to the work of another. Six conditions under which a writer should cite the source of the information are these:

1. The writer uses a direct quotation.

2. The writer copies a table, chart, or other diagram.

3. The writer summarizes a discussion in his own words.

4. The writer constructs a diagram from data provided by others.

5. The writer paraphrases an opinion that he has read rather than reached independently.

6. The writer presents specific information that cannot reasonably be considered common knowledge.

The first four conditions are definite and should cause the writer little problem. The last two, however, are subject to the writer's judgment. They can be resolved by the writer's own experience. During the research she will know which conclusions are those of her sources and which are her own as the results of her own reading. The former conclusions need citations and the latter do not. The writer, however, should heed this general advice: "When in doubt, cite it."

Complete this activity.

3.11   Write *citation* or *no citation* on the blank to indicate which examples need or do not need citations.

a. _____   Lester Thurow suggests the establishment of an education bank as an investment is human capital.

b. _____ $Cx = \dfrac{c^0 1 + x + kx(x + 1)}{2}$

c. _____   After reading you arrive at the idea that coffee grounds rubbed on a wart will make it go away. You decide to use that idea in your research paper.

d. _____   Johnson and Smith disagree on the question of taxation. Johnson views taxation as a real problem; Smith disagrees.

e. _____   Adam Smith concluded "the skill of a man may be regarded as a machine that has a genuine cost and returns a profit."

While he is writing the rough draft of the research paper, the writer may designate places for citations in one of two ways. He may simply paper clip the note card to the written page at the place where the note will appear in the text. He may prefer to write in parentheses the name of the author and the page number of the reference. The object of this exercise is to save time during the writing of the final draft when citations will be placed within the text of the paper. The writer, then, wants to avoid confusion in going back through note cards and bibliography cards to find the author and page number of a source.

Transition. A transition is the natural progression of thought from sentence to sentence and from paragraph to paragraph. Effective transition causes any writing to move smoothly from idea to idea with the connecting ideas relating directly to the thesis statement. A transition might be compared to a bridge that connects one idea to another.

Effective transition is largely determined by the outline. It is also determined by the logical progression of thought within the paper. Transitional elements can also be observed. Words, for instance, provide transition when they are repeated from sentence to sentence or from paragraph to paragraph. Repeated nouns and their pronoun antecedents serve as transitions, although the writer often makes no conscious effort to repeat these words. If he uses a noun, he will undoubtedly repeat it or will use a pronoun in reference to it.

Sometimes the writer will use words or phrases at the beginning or in the middle of a sentence to signal a relationship in thought. Conjunctions such as *and, or, nor, but, for*, are the most common of these markers. Other words serve a similar purpose. If the writer introduces an illustration, he may use *thus, for example, for instance*, or *to illustrate*. To add another phrase with the same idea, he might use *secondly, in the second place, next, moreover, in addition, similarly, again, also*, or *finally*. To show a contrast or a qualification, the writer may use *on the other hand, nevertheless, despite this fact, on the contrary, still, however, conversely*, or *instead*. To indicate a conclusion or a result, the writer uses *therefore, in conclusion, to sum up, consequently, as a result, accordingly*, or *in other words*. These transitional markers are used to connect paragraphs as well as sentences.

This paragraph illustrates the relationship that occurs in a **coherent** research paper.

Another significant cost is the cost of sports facilities. A football stadium may be merely a field with wooden bleachers or it may be a replica of the Vikings' U.S. Bank Stadium. Its cost nevertheless, is part of the cost of the sports program except during the time it is used by participants in the regular physical education program. Similarly, the prorated cost of a competitive gymnasium should be part of the cost of the athletics program. Any other room in the school or any room rented from another source must be counted as part of the athletics cost.

A complete sentence or a short paragraph is sometimes a necessary transition between paragraphs when the relationship between the two is not obvious. In the following example the writer had been discussing the expense involved in high school athletics. As she moved on to discuss the income from school athletics, she needed a sentence to lead into that topic. This sentence is how she could accomplish that aim.

The sports program is not entirely an expense proposition. Income from gate receipts and other sources should help defray the costs of the program. Income is often received from other sources including donations, money from concessions, and profits from the sale of athletics publications such as game programs and picture books.

Complete this activity.

3.12 Show that you know how to use transitional elements by rewriting in the space provided the following sets of sentences into coherent paragraphs.

a. Career planning is essential for all high school students. Students need to understand their strengths and weaknesses. They should learn where their talents lie. They should know career opportunities in the 21st century. They should know which jobs require further schooling. They should know how much the job they are interested in will pay.

_____

_____

_____

_____

_____

_____

_____

_____

_____

b. To ready a pack for backpacking is quite a project. A person needs a stove. One needs food, preferably freeze-dried. He needs to pack a sleeping bag and a rubber pad for under the sleeping bag. He needs matches. He should pack a mess kit. He should have a first-aid kit. He needs a canteen of water. He should have clean clothing.

_____

_____

_____

_____

_____

_____

_____

_____

_____

_____

Diction. Diction in a research paper is more formal than everyday speaking and writing. Research papers are void of dialogue, slang, contractions, and folksy sentences. The reason for formality is that the subject under investigation demands serious presentation. This does not mean that words must be multi-syllabled and scholarly, but they should be precise and should leave little opportunity for misinterpretation by the reader. The research writer should not use contractions such as *can't, don't,* and *it's.* He should, also, write the paper in third person (*he, she, it,* and *they*) and refrain from using first and second person (*I, we, us,* and *you*). Third person achieves the distance from the reader that the writer must maintain in a serious research paper.

Formal sentence structure also keeps misinterpretation to a minimum. Because the research paper is factual, a light-hearted approach to the subject will cause the reader to take the presentation less seriously. The following examples illustrate inappropriate language for a research paper.

Example: Our school's cross-graded multi-ethnic, individualized learning program is designed to enhance the concept of an open-ended learning program with emphasis on a continuum of multiethnic, academically enriched learning using the identified intellectually gifted child as the agent or director of his own learning.

The previous example is so scholarly in language and sentence structure that it is difficult to understand.

Example: Neil Postman gave some neat info. on crazy talk in his book *Crazy Talk, Stupid Talk.* He says that crazy talk is talk that doesn't make sense in the situation in which it's used.

I say, "Right on, Mr. Postman!"

The second example is too informal for a research paper.

Complete this activity.

3.13 Rewrite these sentences so that they will reflect the natural, but formal, writing style of a research paper.

a. The author doesn't care a speck if anyone buys his idea.

_____

b. Skill areas are made up of sequences or hierarchies of skills, the fundamental ones of which are necessarily learned at the earliest stages of development.

_____

c. I agree with Mr. Jones's contention that there is life after death.

_____

d. You should never jog immediately after eating a big meal.

_____

e. Jones said, "I believe unquestionably in greater taxation." Smith replied, "Well, I don't. I think the whole tax structure is ridiculous."

_____

Complete this activity.

3.14 Write the first draft of your research paper.

 CHECK _____ _____
Teacher   Date

Introduction. After the first draft of the research paper is written, the writer composes the introduction and the conclusion. The introduction attempts to get the reader involved and interested in the subject. Many kinds of introductions are appropriate for research papers. Sometimes the writer announces the topic with a challenging question and a hint at its importance.

Example: How can a school district solve two serious budget problems and still be able to provide quality education for its students? The Hometown High School District solved its problem with rising operation costs and declining enrollment while offering a diversified program to its students.

At other times the writer announces the topic and describes a problem in the form of a brief representative incident.

Example: Accurately determining the cost of athletic programs to school districts can be a frustrating exercise. The costs are often inadvertently or deliberately buried in the budget and identifying them becomes virtually impossible.

Another type of introduction announces a topic and indicates the subtopics that are to be discussed.

Example: The concept of human capital has a colorful history. It was first expressed about 1691 when economist Sir William Petty of England termed labor the "father of wealth."

Read these introductory paragraphs and answer the questions.

3.15   Americans are proud of their variety and individuality, yet they love and respect few things more than a uniform, whether it is the uniform of an elevator operator or the uniform of a five-star general. Why are uniforms so popular in the United States?

    a. How is the topic announced? _____

    b. How is your interest aroused? _____

    c. What do you believe the subject will be? _____

3.16   The community comes alive at night! Schools that once were dark in the evening are now alive with lights and people. The people are adults and the lights are on and the school buildings are open because adults are enrolled in community education classes.

    a. How is the topic announced? _____

    b. How is your interest aroused? _____

    c. What do you believe the subject will be? _____

3.17   Carnivorous plants usually eat only bugs or hamburger, but legend has it that some carnivorous plants actually attack and eat people. Whether they do or not is a matter for debate. Carnivorous plants are a challenge to the grower.

    a. How is the topic announced? _____

    b. How is your interest aroused? _____

    c. What do you believe the subject will be? _____

Complete this activity.

3.18   Write an introduction for your research paper.

✓ **CHECK** _____ _____
                         Teacher   Date

Conclusion. The conclusion is the final paragraph that the writer composes. It is important that the writer not merely cease writing when the subject has been thoroughly explored. The reader expects a short paragraph that brings all information together and into focus. That focus is the object of the conclusion. A conclusion does not have to be dry and uninteresting. It may restate or sum up, make a prediction, plead for action, be quiet, or be climactic. These examples illustrate different types of conclusions.

To sum up and make a plea for careful thought and possible future action:

The only way the community will be able to stop bicycle accidents is for each bicyclist to learn the rules for safe riding. The community should also pressure City Council for the installation of more bicycle paths.

To summarize and to point forward:

Slang, then, is derived, clipped, phrased, and used by all peoples of all lands. It can be traced to the earliest cultures. It is the normal language process of word coinage, borrowing, and semantic changes. It is language, legitimate from the standpoint of the linguist, who believes in linguistic realities rather than linguistic ideals.

To restate the main argument:

Our society has advanced from an agrarian-intensive society to a capital-intensive society to a brain-intensive society. It is the latter society that mandates educational involvement in human capital.

Read these concluding paragraphs and answer the questions.

3.19   School districts that have had to cut athletics from their programs because of budgetary problems have saved up to one-quarter of a million dollars. The message seems clear. School districts should discover what sports programs are costing them.

    a. Does the paragraph give a sense of completeness? _____

    b. How is completeness achieved? _____

    c. Does the conclusion summarize, point forward, give a warning, or express a hope? _____

3.20   The tale of "Cinderella" is literally a rags-to-riches story. Cinderella means big money each year for her promoters. As long as children come to Disneyland, as long as parents purchase her products, as long as youngsters see her films and television cartoons, she will make others rich.

    a. Does the paragraph give a sense of completeness? _____

    b. How is completeness achieved? _____

    c. Does the conclusion summarize, point forward, give a warning, or express a hope? _____

3.21   Desert plants, then, need dry, sandy soil. They thrive on little water and lots of direct sunshine. If they are cared for properly, they will bring the grower many hours of pleasure.

    a. Does the paragraph give a sense of completeness? _____

    b. How is completeness achieved? _____

    c. Does the conclusion summarize, point forward, give a warning, or express a hope? _____

Complete this activity.

3.22   Write the conclusion for your research paper.

✓ **CHECK** _____ _____
                          Teacher   Date

Revision. Careful revision is an important part of writing the research paper. Revision can be as extensive as total rewriting, but drastic revision is usually unnecessary if the outline is well formed and has been followed during the writing of the paper. Revision usually includes rewriting sentences that are imprecise or poorly structured or that are confusing to the reader. Revision can also include changing words to more precise and more meaningful words. Occasionally, an entire paragraph is out of order and must be reconstructed.

During revision, the writer should also check spelling and punctuation to make certain that they are correct. A dictionary should be readily available to the writer to check for correct spelling. A reference book on English grammar will be helpful to the student in correcting punctuation and capitalization errors.

Complete this activity.

3.23 Rewrite in the space provided the following paragraph so the structure is improved. This exercise will give you practice in revision.

There has been just as free-and-easy an interborrowing of slang as of legitimate words among various sections of the English language world. No longer do British audiences need a printed glossary to understand an American detective play. "Tough guy," "lay off," "cop," "oh yeah," are among terms that an English police officer hates to admit have gotten into the vocabulary of British youth. Americans have borrowed English terms like "fed up," "swank."

_____

_____

_____

_____

_____

_____

_____

_____

_____

_____

_____

_____

_____

_____

_____

_____

Complete this activity.

3.24 Revise your research paper. Then have another person read your paper for content. Have him suggest ways the research paper might be improved. If you agree, make the changes he suggests.

✓ **CHECK** _____ _____
                 Teacher   Date

WRITING THE CITATIONS

When a researcher writes the first draft of the research paper, she notes where she believes citations are needed. During the revision process, the writer needs to determine which citations are or are not needed in the paper. The documentation of evidence is an important part in avoiding plagiarism. It also allows the reader to consult the listed sources.

There are a number of different styles for writing research papers. The main three are the Modern Language Association (MLA), the American Psychological Association (APA), and Chicago Manual of Style (Chicago). The MLA format for writing papers is what you are learning in this LIFEPAC. The MLA style is generally used when writing papers for English or literature classes. The APA style is primarily used in the areas of psychology and education. The Chicago style is often used for writing history papers. Once you have mastered the MLA style of documentation, you will find it easy to learn others style when required by teachers or professors.

In MLA papers, citations appear within the text of the paper. After an author refers to or directly quotes material from another source, he references where he found the information. This is done by placing the author's last name and the page number from where the material was found in parentheses behind the sentence. Look at how the following information from Beth Moore's Bible study on Esther is referenced:

> Scripture is a "divinely-inspired meeting place where God reveals Himself and invites us into relationship" (Moore 7).

You will note that after the quotation the author's name appears along with the page number where the quotation can be found. If the author is unknown, use an abbreviated form of the title of the selection. For example, if you are referring to a newspaper article entitled "All Good People Read the News," you may shorten your citation to be "Good People" or "News." Your citation will appear at the end of a sentence looking like ("Good People" 12).

The information used to write citations is derived from your bibliography and note cards. This is another reason it is important that you carefully record information on your note cards. For most citations, the author's last name will be followed by a page number. If there is no author, use a shortened version of the title along with a page number. If there is no page number, leave that space blank. When you refer to the author of the text in your sentence, you only need to record the page number behind the direct or indirect quotation.

There are many rules on how to write citations within a paper. You will want to consult a book or website on details regarding the MLA (Modern Language Association) style of documentation. Many reference books contain MLA guidelines. There are also numerous websites that can help you learn how to document such things as websites, anthologies and Bible passages.

Listed below, find some of the more common examples of MLA citations.

A direct quotation with one author:

> "Experts believe that regional and global politics drive up the cost of food aid and slow the delivery process" (Alford 48).

A direct quote where the author is stated in the text:

> Deann Alford wrote in a June 2006 *Christianity Today* article, "Experts believe that regional and global politics drive up the cost of food aid and slow the delivery process" (48).

An indirect quotation:

> Experts working in areas of famine conclude that politics drives up food costs as well as making it difficult to deliver the food to the people needing it (Alford 48).

Complete this activity.

3.25   Write *incorrect* or *correct* on the blank next to the citation to indicate its accuracy.

a. _____   According to a 2005 *Newsweek* article, "At the latest count, 160,000 children in Niger were still suffering from serious malnutrition, and the lives of 32,000 were at immediate risk" (Pape 30).

b. _____   Eric Pape writes, "At the latest count, 160,000 children in Niger were still suffering from serious malnutrition, and the lives of 32,000 were at immediate risk." Pape 30.

c. _____   "A kite flown in a strong breeze will quickly unspool string as it climbs higher. KiteGen Research in Italy aims to turn that action into electricity." (Stoors, 32).

d. _____   Researchers in Italy are flying kites in hopes to turn their research into electricity (Stoors 32).

e. _____   Stoors writes A kite flown in a strong breeze will quickly unspool string as it climbs higher. KiteGen Research in Italy aims to turn that action into electricity. (Stoors 32).

Complete this activity.

3.26   Write citations for your research paper. Have another student check them for correct form.

✓ **CHECK** _____   _____
                Teacher   Date

COMPLETING THE RESEARCH PAPER

The completed research paper contains several parts: a title page, a detailed outline, the body of the paper, and the works cited. Some long research papers also contain a table of contents. All parts should be neatly typed or handwritten in correct form. Sample pages of a research paper appear in Appendix B at the end of this book.

Title page. The title page is a clean sheet of paper with the name of the research paper centered two inches from the top, the student's name centered and approximately in the middle of the page, then centered at the bottom of the page on three separate lines the course, teacher's name, and the date. A sample title page appears in Appendix A at the end of this book.

Detailed outline. The detailed outline is the writer's revised outline in final form. The purpose of including the outline is to enable the reader to scan quickly the contents and to determine the general information that will be contained in the complete research paper.

Body of the paper. The body of the research paper contains the introduction and conclusion, all the researched material, and the citations. The first page of the research paper is numbered at the bottom of the page. All other pages are numbered by centering the page number at the top of the page.

Works cited. The works cited is the final page of the research paper. It is an alphabetical list of all sources used in researching the subject under discussion. All sources in the citations are listed as well as those used by the researcher but not directly cited. The researcher should form his works cited from the bibliography index cards he wrote earlier. All he need do is alphabetize those index cards and type or handwrite the *works cited* page.

Bibliographical form differs somewhat from citation form, although the information contained in the bibliographical entries is similar. The works cited begins with a centered heading. All entries are listed alphabetically according to the author's *last name*. If the source is by more than one author, only the first author's name is *inverted*. Other authors' names are in normal order.

The first line of the *works cited* entry is not indented, but all other lines are indented two spaces. Entries are single spaced, but a double space (one blank line) is left between entries. When more than one book by the same author is listed, a seven space line may be substituted for the author's name after the first entry. Note the punctuation in the following samples. For a sample *works cited* page, see Appendix C at the back of this book. If the material is from a printed or a web source the word *Print* or *Web* appears at the end of the entry.

Buzan, Tony. *Use Both Sides of Your Brain*. New York: E.P. Dutton & Co., Inc., 1976. Print

Chernow, Ron. "The IMF, Roughest Bank in Town," *Saturday Review*, February 3, 1979, 17-20. Web.

Zunin, Leonard, and Natalie Zunin. *Contact*. New York: Random House, Inc. 1972. Print

Complete this activity.

3.27 Write *incorrect* or *correct* on the blank next to the works cited entry to indicate its accuracy.

a. _____ Weber, George. *Uses and Abuses of Standardized Testing in the Schools*. Washington, D.C.: Council for Basic Education, 1974. Print.

b. _____ "City Schools in Crisis," *Newsweek*, September 14, 1977, 62. Web.

c. _____ Alpert, Judith Landon. "Teacher Behavior Across Ability Groups." *Journal of Educational Psychology*. June, 1974, 348-353.

d. _____ Morehouse Laurence E., and Leonard Gross. *Maximum Performance*. Web. New York: Simon & Schuster, Inc., 1977, 35.

e. _____ Halpern, Howard M. *Cutting Loose*. New York Simon & Schuster, Inc., 1977. Print.

Complete this activity.

3.28 Write your research paper in final form.

✓ **CHECK** _____ _____
           Teacher   Date

↻ **Before you take this last Self Test, you may want to do one or more of these self checks.**

1. _____ Read the objectives. Determine if you can do them.
2. _____ Restudy the material related to any objectives that you cannot do.
3. _____ Use the **SQ3R** study procedure to review the material:
   a. **S**can the sections.
   b. **Q**uestion yourself again (review the questions you wrote initially).
   c. **R**ead to answer your questions.
   d. **R**ecite the answers to yourself.
   e. **R**eview areas you did not understand.
4. _____ Review all vocabulary, activities, and Self Tests, writing a correct answer for every wrong answer.

SELF TEST 3

Answer *true* **or** *false* (each answer, 1 point).

3.01 _____ A writer gets the main headings for the outline from the general headings on his note cards.

3.02 _____ In an outline, Roman numerals represent the details in the outline.

3.03 _____ The two types of outlines are topic and sentence.

3.04 _____ The rules for subdividing in a topic outline are different from the rules for subdividing in a sentence outline.

3.05 _____ An indirect quotation is the exact words of the author.

3.06 _____ Only direct quotations are cited.

3.07 _____ When the writer paraphrases an opinion that he has read, he must cite that opinion.

3.08 _____ The writer writes the works cited page of his research paper from the information on his bibliography cards.

3.09 _____ A transition is a bridge between sentences and paragraphs.

3.010 _____ A conclusion the writer forms on his own through his reading must be cited.

Complete these sentences (each answer, 3 points).

3.011 The guide that leads the writer in the writing of the research paper is the _____ .

3.012 Arabic numbers in the outline signify _____ .

3.013 The order of the outline parts should show a(n) _____ .

3.014 Three types of order for the research paper are a. _____ , b. _____ , and c. _____ .

3.015 The thesis statement should be a. _____ , b. _____ , and c. _____ .

3.016 The exact words of the author are _____ .

3.017 Words of the author that are preceded by *that* are _____ .

3.018 Documentation of material of an author which is included in the text is called a(n) _____ .

3.019 The paragraph at the end of the research paper that summarizes or makes a specific point is the _____ .

3.020 A sentence, short paragraph, or a word that connects one idea to another is a(n) _____ .

3.021 The page at the end of the research paper that lists all sources the writer has consulted in his research is the _____ .

Write *C* **if the citation is correct and** */* **if the citation is incorrect** (each answer, 2 points).

3.022 _____ "Aristotle recognized that dolphins and their kin were air-breathing mammals, not fish. He called them porcine pisces—the pig fish—which became *porpoise* in English" (Ellis 37).

3.023 _____ "When a male brown octopus is ready for a fight, its body turns red" (Schur 7).

3.024 _____ "When the octopus is afraid, it turns white." (Schur, 7).

3.025 _____ "Of the world's 19 types of penguin species, 14 are classified as threatened or endangered, meaning that their numbers are low enough to make scientists worry about the species' long-term survival" (Sohn 3).

3.026 _____ "The vaquita—Spanish for 'little cow'—is the world's smallest porpoise, reaching a maximum length of just five feet. (Vanderpool, Tim 70).

Write *yes* **on the line if the thesis statement is effective for a research paper. Write** *no* **on the line if the thesis statement is not effective** (each answer, 2 points).

3.027 _____ Skiing is my favorite hobby.

3.028 _____ Children in families where both parents work are independent and responsible.

3.029 _____ The brain is really something else.

3.030 _____ Juvenile delinquency results from lack of commitment on the part of youth.

3.031 _____ The Vietnam War was an unpopular war.

Write *C* **if the works cited page entry is correct. Write** */* **if it is incorrect** (each answer, 2 points).

3.032 _____ Young, Liz. *World Hunger*. New York: Routledge, 1977. Print.

3.033 _____ Sally Morgan. *Ecology and the Environment*. New York: Oxford University Press, 1995. Print.

3.034 _____ Schmidt, Gary. *The Wednesday Wars* Clarion Press, 2007 Print.

3.035 _____ Maxine Rose Schur. "Radical Reefs." *National Geographic Extreme Explorer*. September. 2008. Pages. 2 – 7. Web.

Write *yes* **if you would cite the item. Write** *no* **if you would not cite it** (each answer, 2 points).

3.036 _____ John Smith contends, "There is life after death."

3.037 _____ A graph that the writer constructed with information from another source.

3.038 _____ Albert Grosset believes George Washington was the first president of the United States.

3.039 _____ A diagram that the writer copies directly from a source.

3.040 _____ Matthew Means said that children must have exposure to the arts to live a full life.

$\frac{74}{93}$ **SCORE** _____   ✓ **CHECK** _____ _____
                                                    Teacher   Date

↻ **Before taking the LIFEPAC Test, you may want to do one or more of these self checks.**

1. _____ Read the objectives. Determine if you can do them.
2. _____ Restudy the material related to any objectives that you cannot do.
3. _____ Use the **SQ3R** study procedure to review the material.
4. _____ Review activities, Self Tests, and LIFEPAC vocabulary words.
5. _____ Restudy areas of weakness indicated by the last Self Test.

GLOSSARY

analysis . . . . Separating or breaking up of any whole into its parts to find their nature, function, or relationship.

annotate . . . . To provide critical or explanatory notes.

anthology . . . . A collection of poems, stories, essays.

bias . . . . Partiality; prejudice.

cardiovascular . . . . Of the heart and blood vessels.

chronology . . . . The arrangement of dates or events in the order of occurrence.

climactic . . . . Of a forceful ending.

coherent . . . . Logically connected.

consecutively . . . . Following in order without interruption.

contention . . . . A statement or point that a person argues is true.

context . . . . The parts of a sentence, paragraph, or discourse that occur just before and after a specified word or passage, and determine its exact meaning.

dialogue . . . . Conversation.

document (verb) . . . . To supply supporting references or evidence.

editorial . . . . An article that states the opinions of people who work for or publish a newspaper or magazine.

edition . . . . The style, size, and form in which a book is published.

evaluate . . . . To determine the worth of something; to appraise.

facet . . . . Any of a number of sides or aspects.

implication . . . . A suggestion.

microcosm . . . . A little world.

objective . . . . Something aimed at or strived for.

paramount . . . . Chief or supreme.

pertinent . . . . Relevant. To the point.

plagiarism . . . . Ideas taken from a source and passed off as one's own.

pursue . . . . To proceed along on a specific course of action.

ramification . . . . A consequence or result.

simultaneous . . . . At the same time.

statistics . . . . Numerical data.

substantiate . . . . To show to be true or real.

vested interest . . . . A special concern in or connection with.

APPENDIX A
TITLE PAGE OF A RESEARCH PAPER

The Complexity of Archaeology

Harrison Mark Jackson

English 11

Mrs. Thomas

November 17, 2015

APPENDIX B

········· **FIRST POSSIBLE FORMAT** ·············

(Step 1) cover or title page if required

Symbolism in Nathaniel Hawthorne's *The Scarlet Letter*

John Anderson

English 11
Mr. Adams
November 6, 2017

(Step 2) thesis and outline page if required

Anderson i

Thesis: _____
_____
_____
_____

Outline:

I.
  A.
    1.
    2.
  B.
    1.
    2.
II.
  A.
    1.

(Step 3) body

Anderson 1

_____ (Blakely 14).

____. _____

____. _____

____. ____

____. " _____

_____ " (Jones 30).

_____. ____

____. _____

____. _____

____. _____

_____. _____

_____ (Bakersfield 100).

Anderson 2

_____ (Blakely 23).

____. _____

____. _____

____. _____

____. " _____

_____ " (Jones 38).

_____. ____

____. _____

____. _____

____. _____

_____ (Bakersfield 97).

Anderson 3

____. _____

____. _____

_____ (Norris 52). _____

____. " _____

_____ " (Gerdes 12).

_____. ____

_____. _____

____. _____

_____. ____

____. _____

_____ (Parker 35).

_____. ____

____. _____

(Step 4) works cited page

Anderson 8

Works Cited

_____
_____
_____
_____
_____
_____
_____
_____
_____
_____

APPENDIX B

(Step 1) no title page required

Anderson 1

John Anderson
English 11
Mr. Adams
November 6, 2017

Symbolism in Nathaniel
Hawthorne's *The Scarlet Letter*

_____. _____

_____. _____

_____ (Parker 22). _____

_____, _____

_____, .

_____, _____

_____, _____

(Step 2) body

Anderson 2

_____ (Blakely 23).

_____. _____

_____. _____

_____, _____

_____, " _____

" (Jones 38).

_____, _____

_____, _____

_____, _____

_____, _____

_____ (Bakersfield 97).

Anderson 3

_____ . _____

_____

_____ (Norris 52). _____

_____, "

_____ " (Gerdes 12).

_____, _____

_____, _____

_____, _____

_____ (Parker 35).

_____, _____

_____, _____

(Step 3) works cited page

Anderson 4

_____ (Blakely 99).

_____. _____

_____, _____

_____, _____

_____, " _____

_____ " (Jones 80).

_____, _____

_____, _____

_____, _____

_____, _____

_____ (Bakersfield 106).

Anderson 5

_____. _____

_____, _____

_____ (Norris 52). _____

_____, " _____

_____ " (Gerdes 12).

_____, _____

_____, _____

_____, _____

_____, _____

_____ (Parker 35).

_____, _____

_____, _____

Anderson 10

Works Cited

_____

_____

_____

_____

_____

_____

_____

_____

_____

_____

_____

APPENDIX B
Sample Research Paper, first page

Harrison Mark Jackson

Mrs. Thomas

English 11

17 October 2015

The Complexity of Archaeology

An archaeologist is a person who helps to protect and understand the record of the past by uncovering information about ancient civilizations. He does this by digging objects out of the ground and then studying them. When an archaeologist uncovers a piece of history, whether it is a vase or an entire city, he is adding a piece to the puzzle that answers the question: what was the past like? In order to find pieces of past civilizations, archaeologists must complete several steps.

There are multiple steps that an archaeologist must take before he starts to dig. An archaeologist's first step is to decide just what it is that he hopes to find (Panchyk 3). Sometimes he will be looking for a specific item. For example, Howard Carter looked for years hoping to find King Tutankhamen's tomb before he actually found it. Other times, the archaeologist has a more general goal that he hopes to achieve. In this case, he would have in mind some bigger, broader questions that he wanted to answer with his finds.

APPENDIX C

Works Cited

Albert, Tony. *Endangered Oceans*. Greensboro, N.C: Carson-Dellosa, 1993. Print.

Bower, Bruce. "Dolphins wield tools of the sea." *Science News* 3 January 2009: 13. Web.

Doffey, David J. *Dolphins, Whales, and Porpoises: An Encyclopedia of Sea Mammals*. New York: Macmillan, 1977. Print.

Earle, Sylvia A. *National Geographic Atlas of the Ocean: The Deep Frontier*. Washington, D.C.: National Geographic Society, 2001. Print.

Gerdes, Louise I., Ed. *Endangered Oceans: Opposing Viewpoints*. San Diego: Greenhaven Press, 2004. Print.

Norris, Kenneth S. et. al. *Whales, Dolphins, and Porpoises*. Washington, D.C.: National Geographic Society, 1995. Print.

Pala, Christopher. "Victory at Sea." *Smithsonian*. September: 46-55. Web.

Parker Steve and Jane Parker. *The Encyclopedia of Sharks*. Willowdale, Ontario, Canada: Firefly Books, 2002. Print.

Perrine, Doug. *Sharks*. Stillwater, Mn.: Voyageur Press, 1995. Print.

Ruvinsky, Jessica. "They're Just Like Us." *Discover*. January 2009: 28-29. Print.

Townsend, Allie. "This Is My Job." *Popular Mechanics*. April 2009: 126-126. Print.